NO MORE BUSINESS AS USUAL

LEADING FROM THE EDGE OF INFINITE POSSIBILITY

By Chutisa and Steven Bowman

Conscious Leadership: The Key to Success, 2005
Prosperity Consciousness: Leading Yourself to Money with Conscious Awareness, 2007
LifeMastery (Aust) Pty. Ltd.

Big Country Publishing, LLC

No More Business as Usual
Leading from the Edge of Infinite Possibility
Copyright© 2012 by Chutisa Bowman and Steven Bowman
ISBN: 978-0-9847831-4-4
ISBN eBook: 978-0-9847831-5-1
Library of Congress 2012931782

This book may be ordered by contacting:
LifeMastery (Aust) Pty Ltd
17 Gordon Grove, Malvern
Victoria, Australia 3144
+61 (0) 3 9509 9529
www.conscious-governance.com

Published By:
Big Country Publishing, LLC
7691 Shaffer Parkway, Suite C
Littleton, CO 80127
USA
www.bigcountrypublishing.com

Because of the dynamic nature of the Internet, any Web addresses or links contained in this book may have changed since publication and may no longer be valid.

Printed in Australia, UK, USA

CONTENTS

ACKNOWLEDGEMENT

Heartfelt gratitude to Gary Douglas for his awareness, guidance, generosity of spirit and for the key to unlocking the energy, space, and consciousness that we truly are.

This book owes its existence to Gary Douglas and Access Consciousness: Empowering People to Know That They Know. Our experience with Access Consciousness tools, processes, and practices were the platform for much of what we have written here. The subject of this book is *no more business as usual*. But perhaps more precisely it is a book about possibility, choice, question, contribution, and what it would take to lead your business and your life from the edge of infinite possibility.

AUTHORS' NOTE

This book is for people who are dedicated to creating a life greater than what they now have and to making a difference in the world. In this book, *No More Business As Usual*, we provide insights into business and life that have arisen out of our work with thousands of executive boards and teams over several decades.

Western economies have entered a new era. We live in a time of accelerating change in the global landscape. Globalization, environmental calamities, technological advances, and other complex forces are buffeting us like never before. To thrive and flourish in these circumstances, we must expand our awareness and formulate generative strategies for our business and our life. The ability to prosper and thrive in tough times is what sets high-profit businesses apart from ones that are barely scraping by.

In this tumultuous business environment, doing business-as-usual is a formula for business derailment and financial meltdown. To prosper and thrive in the decade ahead, leaders have to think differently about reinvigorating their business. They must be willing to let go of all the timeworn conventional business models that keep their business from being remarkable.

In the next decade, leaders must entrain themselves to be more strategic coupled with a greater sense of personal awareness (what we have termed "strategic awareness"), and foster and function from an abundance and possibility view of the world that we have termed prosperity consciousness. These two terms and many more are described and illustrated in detail throughout this book.

Just imagine what your business and your life would be like if you stopped functioning on autopilot and began to generate your business with strategic awareness and prosperity consciousness. This is truly possible—except you have to be willing to change. It takes the willingness to be aware of everything, which allows you to perceive different possibilities. It also requires you to expand your awareness and develop clarity of vision to see beyond this contextual reality. If you have the awareness to know what is happening and where you are going, you will be able to generate something different. With this book you'll get the awareness you need to lead your business in any financial environment!

CHAPTER ONE

Why No More Business As Usual Matters

No-more-business-as-usual is about not being inhibited and restricted by conventional business paradigms or confined by the standard models you have previously abided by. It requires a willingness to generate visions, strategies, ideas, and actions that do not fit the patterns on which you've built your previous success.

The way the world does business has become a burning daily issue in the current economic environment. The nature of business practice is under scrutiny as well. For decades, successful organizations have focused on creating their business by benchmarking the competition and embracing a traditional business model based on competitive advantage. This is one of the key reasons many new businesses never make it beyond the initial levels of business development before they run out of resources.

The role of leadership in business is coming under increasing scrutiny, with calls for more accountability in governance at the senior executive team and board levels. Seldom has a week gone by without a media report of a business that has self-destructed, been called to account for alleged inappropriate use of assets, or criticized publicly due to perceived lack of leadership. There has also been a growing focus on the phenomena of executive derailment, where executives engage in behaviors that cause harm to themselves and their organizations. Like train derailment, executive derailment usually comes as a surprise to everyone, including the executive himself or herself. Business executives who derail have a number of common characteristics, which include difficulty in adapting and changing, problems with interpersonal relationships, inability to build and lead a team, failure to meet organizational objectives, and an overly operational focus that discounts the importance of strategic positioning.

Managing Uncertainty

Things are changing. Making decisions and taking action have become more complex for business leaders in all industries and in all markets. Between financial calamities and environmental emergencies, organizations can no longer conduct their business as they have in the past. Businesses are becoming more multifaceted and changing at a faster pace. Service and product development initiatives must be more efficient and more rapid, and business innovation must be generated more quickly. Attempting to duplicate past achievements, preserve tradition, and keep everything the same can at best create outcomes like those achieved in the past. Doing business-as-usual may, at the very most, keep your business surviving, but at the same time, it prevents your organization from blossoming and flourishing. Normal business practices based on traditional business models are not working anymore. The old way of measuring value is becoming irrelevant.

A business-as-usual model produces mediocre outcomes. Standard business-as-usual practices are designed for survival. They are about getting by. If you are not happy with your circumstances right now, please recognize that you can make new choices and begin to change your circumstances for the better. The sooner you relinquish a business-as-usual mindset, the sooner you'll become truly fit to lead from the edge of infinite possibility.

Maintaining business-as-usual obligates you to stay within your comfort zone and prevents you from going beyond the bounds of what is deemed normal and customary by your sector or industry. You have no choice but to yield to the level of average, unremarkable, mediocre, and run-of-the-mill. If you seek remarkable outcomes and outstanding success, they will not transpire from maintaining a business-as-usual point of view. Remarkable outcomes and outstanding success can be generated only from adopting a no-more-business-as-usual mindset and actions.

The financial downturn and changes in the environmental climate make the development of conscious business everyone's concern. This current environment has been a devastating experience for organizations that have been slow to distinguish and take care of the elemental changes in economic and societal demands. At the same time, there have been abundant opportunities for organizations to practice no-more-business-as-usual. These new times have brought with them an array of opportunities and different possibilities. To seize these new opportunities and possibilities, leaders must be willing to challenge traditional perceptions. They must banish old paradigms and stop assuming we live in a world of scarcity and peril, which is the survivalist mentality of contextual reality.

Contextual Reality Limits the Scope of Your Business Potential

The renowned facilitator of consciousness, Gary Douglas, founder of Access Consciousness: *Empowering people to know that they know*, gives a striking explanation of what contextual reality is:

> *Contextual reality is a reality where you exist only in the context of something else. You are always trying to locate yourself in the structure of what everyone else believes reality is. Contextual reality requires you to be in a constant state of judgment of you because you have decided that the contextual reality is greater than you.*

Leaders who lead based on contextual reality accept as true the idea that other businesses in their chosen industry are their competitors and that they have to beat those competitors to succeed. They assume that life is about competing to survive in a world of scarcity and constraint. For instance, they assume that industry boundaries are fixed and definite, and that the competitive rules of the game must be abided by. They have many experiences that prove their *point of view* about reality is a *fact* about reality. Executives who lead based on contextual reality try to outperform their rivals and grab a greater share of product or service demand. They believe they have to control events and use force and effort to ensure that everything goes the way they want it to go. They believe that control and force are the source of creation.

What You Believe Is What You Create

Your assumptions and points of view about your business determine how you create it, operate it, and relate to it. The way you perceive, judge, and react to events throughout the day is based on your assumptions and points of view, which then anchor you in your view of what reality is. The good news is that you can change your points of view and thus change what you experience. Look at a current situation in your life and your business and ask: What points of view do I have that create my life and my business the way they are?

To see what this means in a business context, consider a discount retail fashion company. The conventional paradigm and mindset of most discount clothing companies has been to milk the most popular style. They do this by finding the current popular style and the best seller this year, take them to Asia, knock them off, and sell them next year in high volume for cheaper prices. This inevitably creates lags in inventory supply and turnover. This is business-as-usual for most discount clothing companies. A great example of a no-more-business-as-usual star is Hennes & Mauritz or H&M fashion retailer, based in Sweden. H&M has demonstrated what could happen when a business changes a point of view from the business-as-usual paradigm. The original brand identity of H&M was a cheap clothing retailer. H&M was known for being of good quality and cheap price. For a long time that was all H&M needed to be. Of course, the garments had to be good enough to satisfy their customer's requirements, but that meant the styles had to be up to date enough, not be fashionably trendy.

In the beginning, H&M used to be all about price, and then they changed their point of view about their business and changed their brand identity from being "just about price" to being "high-end fashion at an affordable price"; They chose to add quality designer fashion to the equation even though conventional viewpoints said it was not possible to combine them successfully. They chose to be contrarian to conventional opinion. H&M is now known for being a temple of "cheap chic" since their merchandise is priced as low as the fashion is trendy. They gained a new reputation for being discount high-end fashion retailers through special one-season-only collections from celebrity fashion designers such as Karl Lagerfeld, Roberto Cavalli, Rei Kawakubo, and Jimmy Choo as well as with trendsetting personalities such as Kylie Minogue and Madonna. Also in 2005, H&M used Stella McCartney to help add style to their collections. With the introduction of these major stylists, H&M was able to increase their market share. H&M has demonstrated that when an organization is willing to let go of a fixed point of view of what it has to be, something even greater can show up.

Be aware of the reality you exist in. There are four major assumptions and conventional premises that most leaders adopt as their strategies. These key assumptions keep them trapped, competing in contextual reality.

Assumption 1: There are inflexible industry structures and boundaries.

Business leaders adopt conventional business strategies because they believe their industry's structural characteristics are inflexible and their business boundaries are defined. They conclude they must compete within these limits or boundaries. The dominant focus of their business strategy then becomes being in context with contextual reality.

If you accept this assumption, you create your business in the context of the industry's structure and you attempt to locate yourself within the structure of that industry. Unfortunately, contextual reality also produces an anti-conscious environment of wide-ranging competitiveness and stress. There's a compulsive need to fit in, to benefit, and to win, accompanied by the simultaneous fear of losing.

The recorded music industry provides a good illustration of an inflexible industry's structure. Until recently the recorded music business fervently defended itself against the changing nature of its marketplace. They refused to recognize and acknowledge that customers preferred to purchase individual songs instead of entire CDs. Music executives refused to allow the public to buy and download individual songs online. These music businesses are now struggling to let go of the business model that made them a lot of money. They are still trying to impose this old model on customers and force them to buy complete CDs, even though music CD sales continue to decline. They are adamant about creating business-as-usual. They create from what they believe in instead of what they are aware of. Their minds are closed to other choices. In their view, there is nothing to question about the way recorded music is sold. There is no other possibility.

In the meantime, many independent musicians are having great success at marketing and selling their music online—the way the public wishes to buy it. Many bands have chosen to forego a record label and instead market and distribute their music only on the Internet. Digital marketing firms such as CDBaby, Magnatune and iTunes offer opportunities such as podcast creation and promotion and video hosting. Services, such as TuneCrank, have been set up to distribute independent music over the Internet with many different types of payment models. This often allows artists to reach a much wider audience than would normally be possible as a local band.

These examples offer several insights into the way one operates in contextual reality. Past references and ways of doing business are seen as significant. Consistency and sameness are considered valuable. For businesses operating in contextual reality, a static environment is seen as an essential foundation for a sense of certainty, security, and safety. When leaders are caught up in contextual reality, they become trapped in the habitual patterns of their beliefs and assumptions. It's a place they are accustomed to; it's familiar. Contextual reality carries certainty and predictability—but no sense of the opportunities that are possible.

Assumption 2: Businesses must specialize and concentrate their efforts in order to excel and establish competitive advantage.

Contextual reality gives leaders a way to define, quantify, and identify who they are. This assumption requires them to be in a constant state of motion to create the context in which they fit, benefit, and win (or lose), and it encourages them to structure their business with highly defined boundaries, limits, policies, procedures, rules and regulations, so things stay exactly the same. They know where they exist in relation to everything else. They are always able to locate their business within that structure and establish competitive advantage in one category.

Potentially great organizations are crippled by leaders who focus on specializing, refuse to be aware of the new hyper-change world and continue to manage their business as usual. Leaders who embrace this second assumption are trapped in the fixed points of view of their past success and they tend to make judgment calls, trade-offs, and compromises that harm their organizations.

For example, in the late 1980s the gross margin on personal computers was 35 percent. However, by the late 1990s it was reduced to about 18 percent. This was an irrefutable signal to an organization like IBM that external change was occurring. However, IBM had been operating with a management philosophy based on the rigid assumption of permanence, which prevented the organization from being able to change at the pace and scale that was required. IBM's leaders refused to acknowledge that their PC industry advantage was declining. They had an extremely rigid form and structure that had built up over decades, which they regarded as highly significant (another fixed point of view). This prevented them from moving beyond the mainframe computers that had been IBM's mainstay for so many years.

IBM had created such a fixed point of view about what its business was that it was unable to be strategically aware of other possibilities. The leadership team was unable to see anything that did not fit its preconceived view of what the business should be. They believed they were running one of the most powerful organizations in the world. Who could have imagined that the leadership team could be blinded by its own success? This fixed point of view caused them to miss the dramatic shift in technology from mainframes to microprocessors. Their market advantage in PCs not only declined; the company never recovered.

In this instance, IBM leaders not only refused to accept the threat of personal computers; they actually contracted their zone of awareness and resisted all effort to see the value of personal computer software. Instead they chose to further cement their position in their traditional products. They continued to operate with an absolute devotion to the "IBM way," which obstructed awareness and prevented innovation. They denied the warning signs that power was moving from hardware to software and refused to reposition their business in the new environment. IBM subsequently sold its PC division to Lenovo of China.

Assumption 3: To succeed you need to beat the competitors.

If you are concerned about winning against competitors, you are operating from the point of view of contextual reality. This mindset induces you to fight for more and to treat others as competitors rather than focusing on what contribution your business can be to your customers, to the community, to the society, and to the world at large. When you choose to concentrate on being a contribution, everything is an endless possibility because you function from a place of generosity of spirit, awareness, and joy. You put your energy where it needs to be, and you are willing to be and receive all energies and no judgment is required. Being a contribution as a business executive is where you are in question, and ask:

What contribution can I be?

What question can I ask?

Is this a contribution to our business, to our customers, to everyone concerned' and to the world at large?

What can I choose here?

Contribution is a being, not a doing. Choosing to be a contribution is the difference between surviving and thriving, where you are not merely making a living but also making a difference. Being contribution, having generosity of spirit, supporting others, and building partnership is critical for building a successful business. When you are functioning from being a contribution, things come together quickly and easily—everything falls in place instantaneously. However, when you're seeking to beat the competitors, you must of necessity do judgment and answer. Operating the business from the need to have competitive advantage requires you to constantly judge whether or not you have got it right yet. What would it look like if your business functioned from contribution rather than competition?

The push to gain a competitive edge is an unquestioned, sometimes even unspoken, defining prerequisite for your business. This point of view becomes a default setting for the way most executives conduct business. They see maintaining their competitive edge as the vehicle to success and operate from the scarcity and survivalist mentality of this reality. They assume that business is about competing, staying alive, winning, losing, and surviving in a world of scarcity and limited possibility. These highly competitive leaders use statistics, competitive benchmarking, surveys, and other tools to determine their place in the context of their industries. Their focus becomes: Where do I fit? Where do I benefit? Where do I win?

Where do I lose? They look to see what others in similar areas are doing and try to out-compete them. They have the point of view that there is a short supply of clients and a limit to opportunity.

Contextual reality creates a world of judgments and beliefs. Much of a company's energy is put into keeping up with or surpassing other companies operating in similar contexts. Business leaders thus trap themselves in contextual reality. Very seldom do they consider another context or ask, What else is possible? When leaders create their business by trying to put it in context with everything else, there is no question, no choice, and no other possibility.

The recent and ongoing example of the financial system meltdown in 2009 is a case in point demonstrating that current business strategies and business practices need to change. Businesses need to cease engaging in head-to-head rivalry based on the scarcity paradigm and the erroneous attitude that success is dependent on fierce competition.

In our view, the problem lies much deeper than a simple financial crisis. The real problem lies in the embedded scarcity paradigm that has underpinned the behavior of the markets. The change in financial market liquidity has driven people to function from of fear of lack rather than creating from the generative energy, space, and consciousness they truly are.

Assumption 4: Successful business is a zero-sum game.

The underlying economic assumption for most business is that we live in a world of scarcity and lack rather than prosperity and abundance, so when one person wins, another loses. When you operate your business based on this assumption of lack you spend your days complaining and worrying about what you don't have enough of. You don't have enough staff, you don't have enough clients, you don't have enough profits, you don't have enough time, and you don't have enough cash. You become trapped in a cycle of frustration, disenchantment, and discontent. What begins as a misguided assumption grows into a giant justification for an unsuccessful business! Through the lens of contextual reality, some would argue that scarcity is the factual, realistic, normal, natural, and inevitable basis for business practice. People who believe this point of view are buying a lie. Scarcity is a lie. The lie of scarcity is the most prevalent and prominent influence in contextual reality. This lie often overrides rational viewpoints and creates distorted, selfish attitudes, and egocentric behavior. When you function from the scarcity and survivalist mentality of contextual reality, you create limitations for yourself and your organization. You feel more secure when you can identify and create the context in which you fit, benefit, win or lose. You are concerned about being in control and you become risk averse, which is another way of saying that you refuse to see opportunity.

This assumption reflects in the way many organizations set their strategy and conduct their business. Since they assume that resources are limited, they tend to speed up, engage in battle, and try to grab their portion now before someone else does. After all, if there are only limited resources, one organization's gain must be another organization's loss. The richer and more successful one business enterprise is, the poorer its opponents must be. Sadly, this assumption continually generates the greed, unease, distrust, and meanness that drive most organizations to make sure that they are not the ones who get left out or trodden upon. This point of view also encourages exploitation that results in abuse, maltreatment, and mishandling.

When you get stuck in this scarcity paradigm, you tend to only see doom and gloom, which prevents you from seeing the opportunities that are always around you. A belief in scarcity stands in the way of your organization's ability to perceive different possibilities. In the book *Unlimited Wealth, The Theory and Practice of Economic Alchemy*, Paul Zane Pilzer points out that the economic assumption that we live in a world of limited resources is fundamentally wrong. Pilzer believes this assumption is the cause of much dispossession and deprivation in the world. He wrote:

> *We live today in a world of effectively unlimited resources, a world of unlimited wealth. In short, we live in what one might call a new alchemic world.... In the alchemic world in which we now live, a society's wealth is still a function of its physical resources, as traditional economics has long maintained. But unlike the outdated economist, the alchemist of today recognizes that technology controls both the definition and the supply of physical resources. In fact, for the past few decades, it has been the backlog of unimplemented technological advances, rather than unused physical resources that has been the determinant of real growth.*

Pilzer also puts forward the idea that business leaders who continue to behave as if they were operating in the old zero-sum world will soon find themselves eclipsed by those who recognize the new realities and take action accordingly. This is one more illustration of how important it is to let go of the business-as-usual paradigm and begin to lead your business from the perspective of no-more-business-as-usual.

While these four assumptions are very common, hundreds of other derivative suppositions keep business executives in a trance; it is as if they are under the spell of contextual reality. These assumptions are insubstantial inferences that exist because of an attachment to and reliance on a false context. Contextual reality induces business leaders to sacrifice what truly matters in exchange for efficiency and expediency. You do not have to take this path. Become aware of the context—and the assumptions will suspend, dissolve, and uncreate.

CHAPTER TWO

Dare to Be Different

You have a choice in life. You can have an extraordinary life (which means you get to have more cars, more houses, more of everything that is valuable in this reality) or you can have a phenomenal life. A phenomenal life goes beyond everything you've ever thought was real and goes to a place where you can create and generate something that's beyond your imagination, beyond your capacity to perceive, beyond your capacity for creation of limitation.
~ Gary Douglas

The recession has weeded out many business players that were stuck in the scarcity and survivalist mentality of contextual reality. In recent years, we have observed that leaders who were content to rise with the tide of the economy have also fallen with it. The big risk today is staying with the herd and copying what others are doing. Not adjusting to the new environment or simply being unaware of other possibilities accounts for many business failures.

In *Billion Dollar Lessons*, Carroll and Mui reveal that since 1981, 423 U.S. companies with assets of more than $500 million filed for bankruptcy. Their combined assets at the time of their bankruptcy filings totaled more than $1.5 trillion. What caused all those failures? Various reasons and justifications have been given. Many of these leaders concluded that their collapse was due to forces beyond their influence and power. However, from our observation, everything boils down to paralysis by contextual reality. These failures could have been avoided if leaders had been aware that they were being paralyzed by contextual reality. Many of the companies that filed bankruptcy did not see that they were about to become obsolete until it was too late. They failed to grasp the ways in which globalization, changes in technology, environmental emergencies, and the new hyper-change world could restructure their industries. In most cases, they couldn't quite fathom that their organization's existence could be threatened.

Most business leaders are content to obey the rules and be in agreement with contextual reality. This is what they are trained to do. Business schools and executive training courses offer frameworks that teach business leaders to operate within the contextual reality. With these frameworks in place, leaders understand where they fit, where they can benefit, where they can win, and how to avoid losing. They tend to find false comfort within the confines of contextual reality. Too often they fail to realize that although they might feel secure, with the business-as-usual mindset in place, they will not be able to generate their business from the edge of infinite possibility.

In the current environment, leaders must be able to make decisions efficiently, quickly, and strategically. They must develop the ability to consciously and effectively deal with uncertainty and risk. Besides being versed in the basics of finance, marketing, strategic maneuvering, and so on, today's leaders have to develop an awareness of all of the contextual elements that surround their businesses. They must be aware when they are creating their business based on contextual reality.

In contextual reality, true success, infinite possibility, and unlimited prospects seem impossible. What if you knew differently? In our view, business leaders must acknowledge that the tendency to conform to contextual reality is deeply ingrained and they must be willing to become aware of those tendencies.

Keeping an Eye on the Big Picture

In the 21st century, the boundaries of business are not precisely defined, and the rules of the game are vague, ambiguous, and often fleeting. Organizations that maintain a strategy and management approach based on contextual reality will not be able to thrive in today's environment. As trade barriers between nations and regions diminish and as information becomes instantly and globally available, leaders must constantly keep an eye on the big picture. But since the big picture keeps changing, they must cultivate an ability to be aware of future trends and how these trends may affect their business. Rather than closing their eyes to forewarning indications and hoping that things don't change too much, they must be willing to break with their own successful conventional practices and discover different ways of seeing the world

They need to ask questions such as: What processes are we using to deal with change? What could happen? What will people need and want in ten years? How could the business of bankers, retailers, manufacturers and trainers change in the coming years?

Chevron, the giant oil company, recently demonstrated what it looks like to embrace no-more-business-as-usual. Instead of focusing exclusively on the core business of petroleum extraction, refining, and distribution, Chevron began to ask: What else is possible? What are other ways to produce energy if the oil wells happen to run dry? Chevron is taking a no-more-business-as-usual approach to renewable energy. They are exploring other technologies that leverage their core competencies. They have set out to find newer, smarter, cleaner ways to power the world with advanced biofuels and other energy-efficient technologies such as solar and geothermal. Chevron is making global investments in renewable and alternative energy and energy efficiency such as cellulosic biofuels, which do not undermine the food supply, and geothermal energy, which will provide new raw materials for fuels, new sources for power, and new benefits for the environment.

How much of your business are you creating
so you can be in the correct context of this current reality?

Being in the correct context of this reality is the same as doing business-as-usual, following the norm, basing your decision on past success or a fixed reference point, aligning yourself with conventional business models—all in an endeavor to achieve winning outcomes. You know you are creating your business based on contextual reality when you are constantly thinking: Where do I fit? Where do I benefit? Where do I win? Where do I lose? As long as you are looking for answers to these questions, you are seeking context. You are looking for the reason why something is occurring rather than being aware. When you function from contextual reality as though it is real, you create limitations in your business. How could attempting to place yourself in the correct context of this reality where your decisions are guided by collective points of view do anything other than position your business to the mean average?

The Tendency to Conform

What is it about contextual reality that makes it so limiting? Ever since we became aware of the force of contextual reality, we have been asking: What is it that is so attractive about contextual reality? What is it that holds our mindset and behavior within a boundary and keeps us under its spell?

We discovered that one characteristic particular to a vast majority of people in our society is the tendency to conform. Most people have a powerful desire to fit in and a strong need to remain in good standing with the group—and they believe that they can maintain their good standing by conforming. This tendency to conform is responsible for keeping people trapped under the fiercely influential force of contextual reality.

Social psychologists have discovered that the tendency to conform is so strong in our society that reasonably intelligent and well-meaning people are willing to go against their own basic perceptions and say something that is obviously wrong. Solomon Asch became famous for conducting what have become known as The Conformity Experiments. Asch devised these experiments to examine the extent to which the need to fit in could affect one's perceptions, mindset, and behavior. The test subject, who had been told that he was going to participate in a vision test, was put into a group with seven other people who he believed were also test subjects. All of the other people were, however, aware of the experiment's objective and had been coached on how to answer the test questions.

The test consisted of the entire group being shown one card with a line on it and then another card with three lines of differing lengths. All

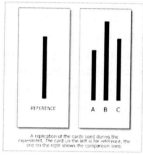

participants were asked which one of the three lines equaled the individual line in length. Asch arranged for the test subject to be the last person to announce his answer so that he would hear other participants' incorrect responses before giving his own. As you can see, the task is simple, and the correct answer is obvious.

A replication of the cards used during the experiment. The card on the left is for reference, the one on the right shows the comparison lines.

Three-fourths of the test subjects in the study deliberately gave the wrong answer in order to conform to the other people in the group. All of those who gave the wrong answer declared after the experiment ended that they knew the right answer, but they chose to give the incorrect answer on purpose.

Why did the subjects conform so readily? When they were interviewed after the experiment, most of them said that they did not really believe their conforming answers but had gone along with the group for fear of being ridiculed or thought "peculiar." A few of them said they didn't want to be different from the rest of the group. Asch was disturbed by these results. He said, "The tendency to conformity in our society is so strong that reasonably intelligent and well-meaning young people are willing to call white black. This is a matter of concern. It raises questions about our ways of education and about the values that guide our conduct."

The Asch experiments provide some vivid, empirical evidence relevant to some of the ideas raised in this chapter. People's tendency to conform is really a wish for status, security, and predictability. They are willing to do whatever they can to fit in and to be in the correct context with everyone else.

What Would You Do?

Imagine yourself in a similar situation as the test subject in this experiment. What would you do? Would you go along with the majority opinion, or would you "stick to your guns" and trust your own awareness? Do you have the courage to stand alone, even in the face of unfavorable consequences? Are you willing to take the necessary social risk to choose for yourself in a group setting? Are you willing to fall out of favor with the rest of the group? Are you willing to be a nonconformist?

Successful business leaders are typically nonconformists even in the face of unfavorable consequences. They have the courage to stand alone, follow their own knowing, and take what others would regard as the risky options while everyone else selects the safe route. In fact, that's a big chunk of what makes them successful.

We have observed that leaders who thrive and meet the challenges of today's hyper-changing environment do not follow conventional business models that are based on contextual reality. Instead, they function from strategic awareness.

Strategic awareness is a space where new ideas and innovation are constantly generated from a heightened non-contextual awareness. With this strategic awareness, leaders operate beyond the goal of competing to actively seize new and different possibilities. They live in the question and act on the possibility of things. They make the improbable or the seemingly impossible come about by bringing awareness and resources to things that lie beyond contextual reality and business-as-usual. This enhances the potentiality and probability of success enormously, ensuring that prospects and possibilities get generated into reality.

Strategically aware leaders have the point of view that there is no short supply of clients and there is no limit to possibility. They are aware that an industry's structural conditions are neither inevitable nor finite. They are able to perceive and find distinctive market positions and sustainable advantages in a multitude of ways. They recognize opportunities and seize them.

Become Aware of the Situation You Are In

People are generally not aware that they have an assortment of beliefs and viewpoints based on contextual reality. As a result, they don't realize that these points of view affect their behavior as business leaders. It doesn't matter how much leadership training you have, if you don't release yourself from the grip of these viewpoints and beliefs, your business won't truly flourish. Your limiting beliefs will have power over your perception and awareness.

If you are experiencing difficulty or a limitation in your business, there must be something you've blocked from your awareness. In fact, if anything in your life is not working, it's because you are unwilling to perceive, know, be, or receive something. That is how your business becomes limited or breaks down. It's the only way your business becomes limited. However, with intensity of awareness, you are able to perceive and receive the changes, positive and negative, that may affect your organization and the world. You trust in your ability to respond to these changes as consciously and skillfully as is required. If you see having this kind of intensity of awareness as a real possibility, imagine what you could create with your business. If you are willing to perceive, know, be, and receive, none of the things that stick you in this reality can exist. On the other hand, you are definitely creating your business from contextual reality...

- *if you spend your time observing the context of your business from the inside out, looking at situations through narrow business or industry lenses that are framed by past reference points.*

- *if you constantly engage in traditional competitive analysis, looking through the lens of your current business practice and industry structure to identify what may transpire in the near future.*

- *if you continue to look backward for a reference point you can use to understand the present.*

- *if you rely too much on the past for indications of what might happen in the future.*

- *if you focus on beating the competition, benchmarking competitors, and trying to out-compete them.*

- *if you assume that an industry's structural conditions are a "given" and you must compete within them in order to succeed.*

Leaders and organizations that operate based on contextual reality are often inflexible in their attitudes. They are restrained, sensible, evenhanded, cautious, consistent, and rule abiding—all terms that imply doing things the way they have always been done. Such leaders tend to require a feeling of certainty and predictability. They tend to waste a lot of time on process, rules, policies, procedures, and structure, and they are frustrated when the desired outcomes are not accomplished. They are afraid of not being in control, and they don't perform well when faced with situations that go against their expectations. They are hemmed in by self-imposed constraints that limit their ability to perceive new possibilities.

Different Possibilities

You have to be willing to change the points of view and beliefs that keep you moored in contextual reality or nothing will change in your business. Since success will require doing new things in different ways rather doing the same things better, would you be willing to perceive, know, be, and receive a new way to look at business? Doing new things in different ways is doing what is unexpected and unpredictable. It's going beyond the norm.

Instead of operating based on what has worked in the past, start generating in the realm of possibility. Give up the question, How can I fix this? and ask instead, What can I do differently that would generate different possibilities? Can you feel the difference in the energy of those two approaches?

When you choose to ask, What can I do differently that would generate different possibilities?, you are no longer constrained by previous successes. You are free to generate something different. As long as you are consumed by trying to do the same things better or committed to making what's not working work, you will keep creating and operating from the same limited set of options.

If you choose incremental improvement instead of doing new things in different ways, you subject yourself to the trap of contextual reality—until you choose to become aware of it and release yourself from its hypnotic power. The less aware you are, the more easily you will be swept along by the force of contextual reality and the less generative you will be in your life and business.

Be aware of the world you exist in. Watch your words, your thoughts, and your energy as you move through the day. Ask yourself these questions:

How much of my business am I creating so I can be in the correct context of this reality?

How much of my life am I creating as contextual?

What benefit do I get from my business being in context with this reality?

If you operate based on contextual reality you will have a tendency to align the practices of present and future business with the practices of the past. You will cling to familiar turf. This will place your organization in jeopardy. Every time you align with the practices of the past, you stop yourself from receiving anything that doesn't match those past experiences.

Once you appreciate this paradox, you will notice its paralyzing effect on almost every aspect of your life and your business. Being captivated by the success of the past can easily destroy your awareness and lock you, contentedly, in place. When you look to the past as a reference point for anything in your future, you will repeat that same pattern as though you are going to get a different result. Or you will pick the pattern from the past that got the best result and repeat it, thinking it will create a better result now. It seldom works because the circumstances are not the same. And even if the circumstances are similar, it doesn't mean you should make the same choice.

For example, if you decide that the past results from your products or services are outstanding, you become unwilling to see when they become passé and outmoded. The moment you judge your products, services, or business model to be right or perfect, you stop perceiving what else is possible. You can't see anything else. You can't perceive or receive any other information. Kodak and Polaroid have made this sort of mistake. They were guilty of seeing the future as a version of their past success rather than accepting that the digital photography revolution could totally change and restructure their industries.

Polaroid had created a revolution with the instant photo industry but it did not keep pace with the emerging digital technology. And Kodak saw the future as a variant of the past and present and couldn't envision how significantly the entire industry was changing. Both Kodak and Polaroid failed to see that the world would go as thoroughly digital as it has. They ignored the likelihood of a significant decline in their business if nothing was done and they avoided radical change. They held on to what they knew and hoped the digital revolution would be short-lived. They were the quintessence of paralysis by contextual reality. Neither company believed in other possibilities. Polaroid declared bankruptcy in 2001, and in 2009, Kodak retired Kodachrome film after a dramatic decline in sales. In 2010, Standard and Poor's removed Kodak from its S&P 500 index.

The future is the source for the creation of your business and your life. Attempting to correct your past mistakes keeps you fixated on the past. You create business-as-usual by looking at the past. You create no-more-business-as-usual by looking to the future. The key is to have gratitude for the past, and excitement and curiosity for the future.

Future Potential

The changes that are taking place globally are unprecedented in their scope. They are generating unlimited opportunities and inimitable threats. If you can perceive these changes as strategic advantages and opportunities, you will be more likely to recognize a new possibility. Certainly, a lot of organizations haven't perceived their future potential and are still doing business-as-usual—in the same old way. But sooner or later, if they don't wise up, they will get an unpleasant surprise.

Business leaders who subscribe to the business-as-usual paradigm cling to familiar territory and habitual behavior. They turn a blind eye toward a changing environment. They often see the business of today and the future as being very much like the business of the past. The truth is change is taking place whether we like it or not. It is prevailing, proliferating, and accelerating. Leaders who function from the no-more-business-as-usual approach are able to harness changes that will lead to amazing growth and unlimited opportunities.

Reflection

> *What are the questions you need to ask to create the business you would like to have?*
>
> *What would it take to shift your focus from being a fierce competitor to being a contribution?*

What would it take for you to perceive the possibilities, not the limitations?

What would it take for you to stop creating your business according to contextual reality and to recognize that you have a different choice?

CHAPTER THREE

No More Business As Usual Is Not An Accident: It's a Choice

Every choice you make determines what your future can be. So when you make a choice, recognize what limitations are being generated with that choice.
~ Gary Douglas

Nobody doubts that the business arena is destined for momentous change. Given the unease created by the global financial crisis, the concern about climate change, and other current events, today's business environment is more volatile than ever. To thrive in an increasingly unsettling and chaotic world, business leaders must become strategically aware and open to change. Great prospects and new possibilities in business always come from changes that are taking place right here and right now. If leaders are blinded by the norms of conventional practice, they won't see the changes until it's too late. Setbacks are certain to emerge when leaders focus primarily on the conventional business-as-usual practices.

Choose to Operate Your Business Differently

The pressure to sustain a flourishing business in a wildly chaotic and frantic marketplace falls on the individual leader. Today leaders are required to be more strategic, more aware, and more flexible, and they must have a stronger decision-making capability. To thrive consistently over the long haul requires discipline and a reliable strategy for dealing with new opportunities and unforeseen adversities. If you're going to out-create and out-perform other businesses, you must choose to operate your business differently.

How? Make the most of your awareness, stop following business-as-usual paradigms, audaciously renounce the status quo, do not take on the limited points of view that other people buy into, and refuse to let bureaucracy stifle your awareness. More importantly, you must not allow yourself to operate within the limitations of this reality or be bound by what is.

Higher levels of conscious choice and intensity of awareness are the keys to creating a balanced integration of organizational vision, and strategic and operational realities. Generating no-more-business-as-usual requires a leader who appreciates the notion of conscious awareness as it relates to business management and practices. They have to transcend their preconceived notions, rise above everyone else's best practices, go beyond all the expert opinions, and triumph over their own doubt. In other words, generating *no-more-business-as-usual* requires a complete transformation on the part of leaders: They must become more conscious. *no-more-business-as-usual* will emerge only with this complete revolution on the part of leaders.

The Power of Conscious Leadership

Conscious leadership isn't about being haughty and supercilious. It's not about lofty or self-important concepts. Conscious leadership is about something much more profound. It's about the capacity to perceive, know, be, and receive the totality of life and the abundant business opportunities that benefit not just one's organization, but all people who are impacted by that organization. This includes the entire workforce, the surrounding communities, and the world at large.

Conscious leaders are generative individuals who exude prosperity consciousness from every part of their being. Prosperity consciousness is where you see the world as an abundant place, where everything is possible, and where you generate from a place of no limitations. Conscious leaders also have a paradoxical blend of intensity of awareness and the ability to think strategically. They are willing to have total awareness of everything that goes on around them without judging anything. From this vantage point, they are able to access real world knowledge of their industry, global trends, and possible futures. They are equipped to perceive and receive all the new opportunities that hyper-innovation, rapid social change, and technological progress generate. We have observed the power of conscious leadership over and over again in all kinds of businesses, large and small. When we see the results of amazingly successful organizations, we know we are witnessing the work of conscious leaders. We have seen that the leadership qualities of chief executives, boards, and leadership teams have a profound effect on the ability of organizations to perform effectively. These leaders have the ability to move beyond logic and analysis and tap into their intuition to make decisions that are bold and innovative. They creatively address issues and have a major impact on the expansiveness of their organization and the people affected by the organization.

The one underlying factor common in these types of business executives is that they choose to be conscious leaders. They are truly aware of what is happening around them and they consciously choose what to do and what not to do. Because of their vision, inventiveness, resourcefulness, nonconformity, unconventionality, creative talent, and generative ability, conscious leaders are sources of substantial transformation for their organizations. The actual business skills they bring to their businesses are much less important than the consciousness they possess, as consciousness will affect everyone impacted by the organization. Put simply, conscious leadership is the key that turns the idea of no-more-business-as-usual into everyday practice.

Limited by the Status Quo

Today, the majority of CEOs and business leaders know that it is imperative to be strategically nimble and dynamically innovative. They know they must be able to inspire their people to perform and be the very best of themselves in every moment. So, why are many CEOs and leaders still captives of the conventional business-as-usual paradigm? There are three likely explanations.

First, most business leaders don't know how to lead with true strategic awareness and prosperity consciousness. They don't see themselves as conscious leaders, and, more importantly, they don't believe that it is possible for them to be that.

Second, most executives these days are appointed into leadership positions by virtue of their technical skills, knowledge, and education. Seldom are people chosen to become leaders of an organization because of their leadership qualities and ability to lead with conscious awareness. In most organizations, "leaders" are in fact managers working under a leadership title. They are selected, trained, and rewarded for their skills and their ability to maintain the status quo and deliver more of the same.

Third, many executives still believe that to be successful they have to create their business to keep them in context with this reality. They have little reason to believe it could be otherwise. They are constrained by the range of feasible choices because they assume that industry boundaries are fixed and definite and the competitive rules of the game must be abided by. Whether these constraints are true or illusory (mostly the latter), they offer executives a comforting justification.

In pursuit of competitive advantage and keeping the business in context with this reality, leaders have to contract their awareness and push infinite possibilities out of sight. They are not able to see beyond current realities, perceive other possibilities, or sense the weak spots or dilemmas that their organization may encounter. They are the effect of life, not the cause.

However successful the current business may be, if leaders constantly contract their zone of awareness, they will not be aware of the choices and possibilities that are available to them.

Choice Creates Awareness

So, if you choose to have no-more-business-as-usual, you are going to need to change your point of view. It takes choice, awareness, ingenuity, and perseverance to generate no-more-business-as-usual.

The main way to master the art of no-more-business-as-usual is in the way you use your power of choice. Choice is the way to navigate change. Every choice you make creates awareness and determines what your future can be. Every moment is a choice between staying with the conventional business-as-usual paradigm—and stepping into no-more-business-as-usual. Whenever you make a choice—any choice—recognize what limitations and possibilities are being generated with that choice.

Have you ever asked yourself what are your points of view about leadership and business practices? In our experience, few business executives have given much thought to the points of view that underlie the way they create their reality and their business.

If you're like most business leaders, you have many points of view about leadership and business principles that you're not even aware you have. These points of view could even be the cause of many of your so-called business problems. Before you set off in search of no-more-business-as-usual, you need to take a moment to become aware of your points of view about leadership and what it takes to run a successful business. You also need to become aware of how these points of view may limit your organizational performance. You will be a victim to your points of view if you are not aware of them.

A conscious leader is the source of an organization's success,
joy, glory, and prosperity.

Discover What Is True For You

To create space for you to instigate no-more-business-as-usual and to lead with conscious awareness, you will need to become aware of your points of view that are based on contextual reality and recognize business orthodoxies that blind you to different possibilities.

Here's how to get started. Ask yourself this question:

What does leadership mean to me?

Write down anything that comes up for you, even if it doesn't make any sense. Unusual or atypical answers could indicate your deeply held beliefs and fixed points of view about leadership and business orthodoxies.

Now take a good look at your responses to the question: Does your answer make you feel lighter? Or does it make you feel heavier?

If your answer is true for you, you'll feel lighter. If it's not true for you, you'll feel heavier. Please recognize that much of what you have learned and bought from the conventional business-as-usual paradigm is what makes you feel heavy.

Let's say your answer is something like: "Leadership is about controlling or managing and about developing an ability to activate compliance and force out immediate results." Does the answer make you feel lighter or heavier? It will probably make you feel heavier because, contrary to what a lot of people think, leadership is not about controlling or managing. It is not about having power over people. Control is an illusion, and the need for control generates never-ending predicaments and misconduct in the workplace. This is one of the most subtle misapplications of the notion of leadership.

Traditional leadership models seek to preserve the status quo and make good "soldiers" of the team. These models train leaders to think their job is to tell others what to do. That is, leaders are supposed to have all the answers. They are expected to appraise others and tell them how to conduct themselves and perform, and ultimately those others are expected to do what they are told. But what if leadership is not about authority, hierarchy, exclusivity, and separation between management and staff? What if leadership is about empowering others rather than having power over them? Does it make you feel lighter to think that this is what leadership is all about? Or does it make you feel heavier?

To break out of the entrapment of the business-as-usual paradigm, you have to be able to discover what is true for you. You have to be able to distinguish between points of view that are generative and points of view that are contractive. Remember, if a point of view is generative for you, you'll feel lighter. If it's contractive and not true for you, you'll feel heavier.

Before we continue, there are other very important questions to ask yourself :

- *What does leadership mean to me?*

- *What does it mean to be a conscious leader?*

- *What kind of leader am I now?*

- *What kind of leader do I want to be?*

- *Am I already a conscious leader?*

- *Do I have conscious leadership potential?*

- *Do I have a sincere aspiration to become a conscious leader?*

- *What would it take for me to run a successful business?*

Reflect on your responses to the above questions. Are you willing to see that it's not what is in the world that limits the pace and scope of your leadership ability—it's your unexamined points of view? Your point of view creates your reality. Before we move on, ask yourself:

Am I aware of how my points of view may limit me and my organization's performance?

What can I do about them?

What needs to change?

Being a leader is not the same as acting as one,
and calling yourself a leader is not the same as being one.

Many leaders we have worked with feel that being "good" is acceptable, and this is as good as it will get for them. They cannot imagine that they are gifted enough to achieve extraordinary levels of conscious leadership. They misidentify that conscious leaders are special, brilliant people, who have been endowed with a unique gift. What if the truth is that we all have been endowed from birth with the same special gift? What if we all have infinite potential to be a truly extraordinary leader if we choose?

Sure, some people are more conscious and aware than others, but in the chaotic and volatile business environment, hardly anyone truly lives up to their conscious leadership potential. Why? Because most business executives haven't been given the tools and space to exercise their gifts. More importantly most executives are not aware of the true power of conscious leadership. The majority of people are so disconnected from their own states of consciousness that they are not aware that it is possible to actually experience this state. Sadly, they do not even realize that the state of pure consciousness is the true essence of their beingness. As a result, they often dissipate an astonishing degree of their awareness.

Start With Yourself

As facilitators and advisors, we know that the moment executives take the initiative to become aware of their limitations, habits, and unconscious conditioning: they are on the path to becoming conscious leaders. Over and over again, we have observed that when business executives do not take the important step of examining themselves, they can be blinded by their limitations. Conversely, by becoming more conscious and aware in their personal self-leadership, not only do they gain greater insight about themselves, they are also able to receive themselves differently.

You cannot generate no-more-business-as-usual until you first become a conscious leader of your own life. This is exemplified by the well-known quote from Mahatma Gandhi, "Be the change you wish to see in the world."

Most people think the power to change and transform means making something happen, which is controlling and forcing it into existence. What the power to change and transform actually means is being aware of where you can put your energy on something you can change, if you want to change it. To be the change you wish to be and to escape the vigorous pull of this contextual reality, you need to become a conscious leader. The problem is that few leaders have the discipline and willingness to step up and become more than they have been willing to be. Yet that's what is required. If leaders are willing to be conscious, they can change anything. Without consciousness, they can't get there. Consciousness is at the core of both personal and organizational growth and expansion. Conscious leaders are able to establish infrastructure that encourages growth of consciousness potential in individuals and groups that will provide exceptional benefits to both. Conscious leadership is the key to creating a balanced integration of organizational vision, strategy, operational realities, and a culture of consciousness.

Consciousness is a way of connecting
what is happening at the present with the infinite possibilities

It's Just Choice

Choice is the source for everything in your life. The things you choose are the source for what occurs in your life.
~ *Gary Douglas*

Be willing to be a conscious leader in the world, and everything is possible. An example of one of the great conscious leaders of the 20th century is Mahatma Gandhi. Gandhi's influence extended beyond India to the rest of the world. His philosophy of non-violence inspired millions; including the great American civil rights leader Martin Luther King, Jr. Gandhi knew that the only resolution to hatred, ignorance, and fear was awareness, openness, truth, and forgiveness. He was determined that, no matter what it took, he was going to change the world. Each and every person he came in contact with became different because of him.

Gandhi changed the world by consciously choosing what expanded every aspect of reality. He didn't just choose what worked for him. For example, when he accidentally dropped a sandal out of a moving train, instead of lamenting his loss, he immediately threw out the other so whoever found them would have a pair. He was able to perceive and receive the inherent greatness of all individuals, regardless of their caste, religion, gender, or social position. Through his conscious choices and his personal and public actions, he was able to promote religious harmony. Gandhi is a beautiful expression of conscious leadership.

Expanding Your Awareness

An important feature of conscious leadership is the capacity to get beyond the limitations of contextual reality. Conscious leaders seek to become aware of the boundaries that define conventional practices, predictable routines, conformist behaviors, and business-as-usual approaches—and then deliberately step beyond them. They have the ability to see beyond the contextual system and determine what they would like to generate. This is not about eradicating contextual reality or getting outside it. It is about rising above it. It is about generating business in the realm of infinite possibility. To wrap your mind around this new way of functioning and being requires you to expand your awareness.

The point is this: If you would like to achieve financial success with your business in today's environment, you need become a conscious leader in your business as well as your life. You actually have to embody conscious leadership. You have to be willing to move out of everything you ever thought was real, everything you thought was true, and everything you have been sold, told, or learned. You have to let go of the business-as-usual paradigm. When you move beyond that, a whole new universe opens up to you. It's just a CHOICE!

Conscious leadership has to do with a new sense of equilibrium and balance between:

- *Inner and outer leadership*

- *Personal growth and business growth*

- *Embracing the vision and empowering others to achieve it*

- *The head and the heart*

- *Executive management skills and conscious leadership abilities*

Going beyond the limitation of contextual reality requires superb levels of self-awareness. To become a truly conscious leader, you must start with yourself—conscious leadership comes from within. It begins with an inner state, which creates a progression of external behaviors. Careful self-examination and a sincere willingness to expand your awareness will provide the foundation for you to become a conscious leader.

In this chapter, we've described what we perceive to be the primary practices that facilitate change and transformation. If you wish to ally yourself with this state of being and the remarkable capacity for change, there must be an essential shift in your awareness, your points of view, and your mindset. This shift in orientation requires new practices and the willingness to choose differently. We have discovered that the greatest challenge for most business leaders lies not in adopting this new business paradigm, but in perceiving that it is truly possible to constantly live and lead with conscious awareness. It's a completely new way to be. Most leaders were well trained and programmed to make themselves and their businesses conform to contextual reality. It's not easy to give up the habit of operating from contextual reality and move into living from the edge of infinite possibilities. So, what needs to change?

Reflection

Are you currently living and operating from conscious awareness?

Are you willing to step up and become more than what you have been willing to be?

CHAPTER FOUR

What if you Were a Conscious Leader?

Consciousness is the ability to be present in your life in every moment, without judgment of you or anyone else. It is the ability to receive everything, reject nothing, and create everything you desire in life—greater than what you currently have, and more than what you can imagine. What if you were willing to nurture and care for you? What if you opened the doors to being everything you have decided it is not possible to be? What would it take for you to realize how crucial you are to the possibilities of the world?
~ Gary Douglas

Consciousness is correlated to the intensity of our awareness and the intensity of our connection with ourselves. It is also inextricably linked with our acknowledgement of our unlimited talents and abilities and our capacity to be in communion with all things. This communion is perceiving, knowing and receiving everything without judgment or limitation. It is an ability that everyone has but few choose. Ultimately, consciousness is a way of connecting with what is happening at the present moment and with the infinite possibilities that are always available.

Consciousness resides inside each of us as an infinite reservoir of intrinsic knowing, wisdom, and acumen. If claimed, owned, and embraced wholeheartedly and sincerely, consciousness allows us to revel in our own greatness and extraordinariness without a sense of superiority or self-importance. Consciousness is our intrinsic faculty and inner resource. Like any other intrinsic faculty, it can be strengthened through choice, practice, sincerity, and fortitude. Being conscious is an experience of expanding our awareness beyond its present limits. It is a state of flexible awareness, with no fixed points of view. When we choose consciousness, those around us share the rewards.

We all have an inner urge toward living more naturally with an ease that is free of disharmony, trauma, and drama. However, the majority of people are so disconnected from their own states of consciousness that they are not aware it is possible to actually experience this state. For most people, everyday living is a struggle due to our strong attachment to anti-conscious habits from past programming. This attachment to anti-conscious habits causes us to be quite disconnected from our own awareness of our choices and infinite possibilities.

Businesses that are directed by conscious leaders tend to function effortlessly, capitalizing on the awareness, creativity, vision, and acumen of individual employees and stakeholders. There is less discord, internal friction or conflict, along with greater fortitude and flexibility in the face of unexpected predicaments, crisis, or calamity.

> *What would it be like if you embodied so much consciousness in everything that you do, that others chose to become more conscious as a result? The magic in your life is created from the true magic of you, which is the presence of you.*
> *~ Gary Douglas*

Energetic Entrainment Frequency

Most of us don't realize how much our consciousness influences other people's behavior—and many of us are unaware of how obstructive and disruptive our unconsciousness and anti-consciousness can be. When leaders expand their zone of awareness, they create a stirring of energetic entrainment throughout their organization.

Recent scientific research from the fields of chaos theory and quantum mechanics has shown that everything and everyone in the universe, including our every thought and every attitude, gives off a vibration or a frequency, and that we are all connected through energy. Another way of saying this is that there is consciousness in everything. We are broadcasting stations radiating our energetic signals to the world. Each person has a particular frequency or vibration—a consciousness or energetic signal—that we radiate or transmit to the environment and other people. It is a composite of the particular frequency or vibration of our body, our mind, our heart, and our consciousness. Each being has the ability to control his or her vibration. Just as you adjust your radio to a particular station by adjusting its frequency, you can attune to higher energetic vibrations by expanding your consciousness.

People who are truly conscious and aware have an energetic empowerment presence that creates an energy field of healing, nurturing, caring, creativity, expansiveness, and joyfulness. This energy field has what is known as an energetic entrainment frequency, which strongly affects others. Entrainment can be defined as the tendency for two oscillating bodies to lock into phase so that they vibrate in harmony. The principle of entrainment is universal. It appears in music, biology, chemistry, pharmacology, medicine, psychology, sociology, astronomy, architecture, and many other disciplines.

The history of entrainment is linked to findings of the Dutch scientist Christiaan Huygens (1629-1695). While working on the design of the pendulum clock, Huygens found that when he placed two clocks on a wall near each other and swung the pendulums at different rates, the pendulums would eventually end up swinging at the same rate. This also occurred when a room was filled with grandfather clocks of different sizes and pendulum lengths. The clocks became synchronized with each other by sending and receiving minute vibrations through the walls and floor of the building.

Not only was energy being transferred; the individual clocks altered their "behavior" in order to become synchronized with the other clocks. Equally noteworthy is the fact that the slower clocks picked up their pace to become synchronized with the fastest (highest frequency) clock. This "entrainment" process has been replicated over and over through the centuries, and has given rise to many scientific and arts-related disciplines.

The fundamental function of each and every one of us is expanding and contracting our consciousness. Are you aware that you always have the experiences, perceptions, and awareness appropriate to your consciousness and vibration level? When you are totally conscious, you have a perception of full awareness, of being in communion with all of life. However, when you are totally contracted and unaware, you become unconscious, energy dense, and resistive of everyone and everything. This wisdom reminds us of the parable of the rainmaker, told by Carl Jung. Here is the parable:

A certain province in China where the missionary Richard Wilhelm lived, was suffering a terrible drought. They had tried all the usual magical charms and rites to produce rain but to no avail. There had not been a drop of rain and the situation became catastrophic. Then someone said there was a rainmaker in a distant province who was known to be effective in producing rain. The local dignitaries invited him and sent a carriage to bring him to the drought-stricken area.

In time the rainmaker arrived and was greeted by the local dignitaries, who pleaded with him to help produce rain. The rainmaker closed his eyes, breathed in the air, then opened his eyes, looked around, and pointed to a small cottage high up on the side of a mountain. He asked if he could reside there for a few days. The officials agreed and the rainmaker went up and locked himself in the cottage. Three days later storm clouds gathered and there was a torrential downpour of rain. The inhabitants were jubilant, and a delegation, led by the officials, went up to the cottage to thank the rainmaker. The rainmaker shook his head and said, "But I didn't make it rain."

The officials said he must have done it, as three days had passed since he arrived in the village and rain had been produced. The rainmaker replied, "Oh, I can explain that. I come from a country where things are in harmony with the universe. We have sunshine, we have rain. Here things are out of harmony, they are not in accord with the order of the universe, and I too was disturbed. I went to the cottage to set myself straight and once I was back in harmony, the rain came naturally."

Like the rainmaker, when you expand your intensity of consciousness, you expand your energetic empowerment, and create a stirring of energetic entrainment throughout your organization. You become the source of an organization's success, joy, glory, and prosperity. When you choose consciousness, those around you share the rewards.

Be the Vibration of Generative Life

Every molecule is a generative element unto itself, which is why chemicals put together create different "reactions." If you are a generative element in the world, you are the catalyst for change and transformation. The potency of life is the ability to be the catalyst for the change and transformation of all things and everyone.
~ Gary Douglas

At the heart of quantum physics is the discovery that everything is connected and that things exist through their relationships. Every component of a system has the potential to affect all other components. You cannot move without influencing everything in your universe. You cannot even observe anything without changing the object and yourself. This means that in order to generate space for no-more-business-as-usual, you need to expand your vibration level and become a catalyst for change and transformation.

In business as in life, if leaders are a catalyst, if they are the chemical that changes everything else, they create an inevitable reaction in their business. The business responds to what they are being. All leaders can have a catalytic capacity. They can transform and change people around them with the questions they ask and the things they do and say. Being the vibration of generative life is a process of *being*, not *doing*. It is the willingness to be an energy that cannot be confined, defined, or limited. This requires dedication and the willingness to become the greatness of who you truly are. If you function as anything less than that, you are choosing to be less than who and what you can be.

Most people try to generate their life and business based on the points of view that define contextual reality. But to truly generate our life and our business, we have to let go of the standard life—the life that meets the standards of everyone else. We have to be willing to let go of this reality instead of trying to bring everything back to the solidity of what we have decided is real.

To expand your vibration level and become the catalyst for change and transformation, you have to expand your zone of awareness. Awareness is the capacity to know everything. It is a continuous, ever-moving, ever-expanding possibility. It is the ability to be totally present in life without judgment of anything that goes on. It is also the willingness to receive in totality the abundance and exuberance of life. The zone of awareness is a real psycho-physiological experience that each of us can choose to have right now. It is like a spherical atmosphere, where everything is in constant movement around us. This is the realm of infinite possibility.

With an expanded zone of awareness you emanate an energy field of healing, nurturing, caring, joyfulness, fun, expansiveness, and an intensity of infiniteness. The keys to expanding your zone of awareness are:

- *Be in the moment, aware, joyful, and mindful. As you go about your daily life, focus more on what you are being than on what you are doing.*

- *Dis-identify from the mind. Expanding the zone of awareness means rising above thoughts, feelings, and emotions. Every time you stop identifying with the mind, your zone of awareness expands. And every time you identify with your mind, thoughts, feelings, or emotions or define yourself in a particular way, you automatically contract your zone of awareness. When you go into your mind to "figure things out," you inevitably begin to function from a limited point of view. You define everything according to a linear viewpoint that is a solid physical mode. You will not be able to expand your zone of awareness as long as you identify with your mind. Would you be willing to recognize that there is a vast realm of infinite intelligence beyond the mind and beyond thought?*

• *Be willing to be out of control. Being out of control is not being uncontrolled. It's not being drunk, disorderly, or illegal. Being out of control means nothing controls or stops you—and you don't need to stop or limit anyone else. When you are out of control, you are willing to function outside of contextual reality and conventional points of reference. It's about not letting the controls of other people's points of view, realties, judgments, and decisions be the controlling factor in your life. Being out of control is being totally aware. You don't try to control the way things are generated. It is only when you are not being totally aware that you try to control what occurs, what comes in and goes out.*

• *Be open and willing to receive everything with gratitude and without judgment. If you wish to expand your zone of awareness, you have to be willing to receive everything. Receiving involves no resistance; it is about remaining constantly open, vulnerable, and unresisting to any energy. Please recognize that whatever you can't receive becomes a limitation. Whenever you are unwilling to receive any energy, you contract your zone of awareness and begin to function from separation, judgment, expectation, projection, and rejection. When you are unwilling to receive, you withdraw from being in communion with others; you withdraw from all things.*

• *Create your life as a celebration instead of obligation, trauma, and drama. Celebrate where you are in this moment and have gratitude for the rightness of yourself. Gratitude is a way of celebrating the rightness of whatever is in your life and creating more space for infinite possibilities to come your way. If you are not constantly expressing gratitude for what you have, you will stop that flow of what can come to you. Celebrate your uniqueness—and you increase your bliss and joyfulness. It is all choice. You are an unlimited being, and as such, you have the power to create the reality you want.*

Embrace a Conscious Awareness Way of Being

How do leaders become truly conscious? We believe this comes about when they choose to become more than what they have been willing to be. We have personally discovered that conscious leadership is about allowing our inner leadership qualities to come forth. This requires us to live in the world as the greatness we are, which then invites everyone else to be the greatness they are.

So, how can you embrace conscious awareness as a way of being in your own life? First, you must realize that consciousness is a choice, just as unconsciousness and anti-consciousness are choices. You will begin to become conscious the moment you choose to be conscious. Consciousness is about right here, right now. It occurs in the moment you choose to be all that is possible.

Choosing to be conscious and aware is completely internal. That is, it has nothing to do with anything or anyone else. It is a commitment you make to yourself not to live by anyone else's judgment and reality ever again, no matter what. This, of course, works only if you are sincere and willing to be aware. The first question to ask is: Do I have a sincere aspiration and willingness to be conscious and aware? The answer can only be *yes* or *no*, because wishful desire does not provide the fertile inner ecology required for conscious awareness to expand. Sincerity and willingness are essential. They facilitate the expansion of conscious awareness by motivating you to choose it.

Your level of consciousness is correlated to the intensity of your connection with yourself, with your acceptance of your unlimited talents and abilities, and the resulting expansion of your ability to be in communion with all things. Being conscious is the very process of expansion; it has nothing to do with new age concepts, the latest fads, or any beliefs about "should" or "shouldn't." The key point about consciousness is: You have consciousness, you are consciousness, and you have a choice to be consciousness. You have to choose to be consciousness; it's not a place you go to—it is who you are.

You must claim, own, and acknowledge it and have it in you. That which you do not have in you, you cannot have at all. If you see consciousness as external and not part of your beingness, you will never have it at all.

Your true potency can only derive from your ability and willingness to be totally conscious. "Truly in consciousness" means you don't have any point of view about anything. It is the ability to receive everything, to judge nothing, and to allow the entire universe to be what it is. You're willing to let anything occur that occurs. If you are willing to give up having a point of view, you can be truly in consciousness. From this space you can transform and change all things.

Each time that you choose to expand your awareness, you change the world into a place in which people can live with total awareness, unbridled joy, and infinite abundance. Every being in this world is affected by the choices you make. You have the power to make an incredible difference. The difference you make can be a magnificent, affirmative contribution, particularly when approached with dedication to conscious awareness, or it can be a negative influence when it is based in unconscious or anti-conscious thoughts, feelings, and behaviors. When you are being the energy of a generative, conscious life, you have the ability to re-adjust every choice you make. No choice is solid or fixed in place. You are aware of what must be dealt with and what doesn't have to be dealt with

Reflection

Can you imagine what it would be like to do everything from the place of consciousness that invites the whole world to function with you, not against you?

Eight Attributes of Conscious Leaders

We have distilled eight attributes of conscious leaders and presented them below. Whenever you are in the presence of a truly conscious leader, you will find these eight qualities. Many business leaders, entrepreneurs, investors, and traders have discovered these eight attributes and applied them to achieve phenomenal success. These eight attributes will allow you to see new possibilities in your business, your career, your organization, your products, and services. The remaining chapters of this book are dedicated to exploring each of these eight attributes.

1. Conscious Leaders Lead From the Edge of Infinite Possibility:

Conscious leaders recognize that they have infinite choice and infinite possibilities at all times. They are always aware of the energy around them and they choose from what is going to expand their business and their own universe. They are willing to connect with their businesses and to direct it, but they don't try to control it. They trust in the flow of the universe and perceive the abundance in all things. (Chapter 5)

2. Conscious Leaders Have Intensity of Non-Contextual Awareness:

Conscious leaders have intensity of awareness. They are able to perceive, know, be, and receive everything without judgment. They inspire others to act. Intensity of awareness allows them to function from a high level of power and renewal because they actualize empowerment and consciousness. Rather than trying to force respect through taking stances or adopting fixed points of view, they generate the potency, palpable presence, and inner-knowing that draws respect and collaboration. (Chapter 6)

3. Conscious Leaders Master the Art of Being "Interesting Point of View":

Conscious leaders are willing to let go of the need to maintain the rightness of their point of view. To them, everything is just an interesting point of view. They are not tied up in what they think or what others think, and therefore generate space for fresh ideas and new possibilities. When everything is just an interesting point of view, leaders start to create choice. By mastering the art of Interesting Point of View, conscious leaders have infinite possibilities. They can be, do, have, create, and generate anything-and they'll have no point of view about it. (Chapter 7)

4. Conscious Leaders Unshackle Themselves From Contextual Reality:

Conscious leaders operate beyond the bounds of contextual reality and see life as an extraordinary adventure. They are unconstrained by the concern for survival and they are free from the generalized assumptions of scarcity. They stand in the great space of infinite possibility in a posture of openness, with an unrepressed imagination for what is possible. They are open to all possibility and sincerely willing to look at what they can do to generate different possibilities. (Chapter 8)

5. Conscious Leaders Are Functional Within Contextual Reality:

Conscious leaders set in motion a spirit of conscious leadership that nurtures the courage to break new ground and the boldness to go beyond limitations, narrow-mindedness, and insularity. At the same time, they are totally aware of the confines of contextual reality that others try to impose—the government regulations, the policies and procedures, the legal requirements, the contractual conditions, and so on. They make conscious choices moment to moment based on the information and awareness they perceive, and they view contextual reality as a playing field to interpret and manipulate in order to create the change they desire. (Chapter 9)

6. Conscious Leaders Are Able To Change And Transform on a Dime:

Conscious leaders are capable of changing the world and transforming the people around them. They are willing to be agents of change. They are not attached to convention and are prepared to take risks and destroy and uncreate old systems, structures, and routines in favor of more expansive ones. They are aware and mindful, ready to shift strategy and tactics as the situation requires. They are willing to be vulnerable and to stay open to the new, the unfamiliar, and the unknown. (Chapter 10)

7. Conscious Leaders Embrace the Magic of Strategic Awareness:

Conscious leaders have superior strategic awareness and the ability to access knowledge and information beyond what is known in the world at the present time. With advanced strategic awareness, leaders are able to capture new opportunities before people who are mesmerized by contextual reality. They are aware of the new possibilities, they conceive of new ideas, and they develop strategies to bring those ideas into existence. They are more likely to see trends outside their industry that could affect the positioning of their business, and they generate new growth opportunities. (Chapter 11)

8. Conscious Leaders Operate Beyond the Bottom Line:

Conscious leaders embody the energy of benevolent capitalism. They operate their business with clearly expressed values and model the benefits of benevolent capitalism and corporate social responsibility. They create a higher playing field for their business. They have ability to generate significant profits for their shareholders while realizing affirmative societal benefits and positive environmental impacts for the world at large. (Chapter 12)

CHAPTER FIVE

Leading From The Edge of Infinite Possibility

The only way of finding the limits of the possible is by going beyond them into the impossible.
~ Arthur C. Clarke

Contextual reality defines everything according to what is possible—and what isn't. Mostly it boils down to this: Nothing is possible apart from what already exists. What already exists, meaning the limitation and connection to contextual reality, is all that exists now and forever. Infinite possibility seems impossible to many people because it disputes their fundamental sense of reality. At this point we invite you to sneak a quick look at what is regarded as one of the most unfathomable parts of the universe: infinite possibility. Infinite possibility exists as generative energy, space, and consciousness simultaneously everywhere and in everything. Every particle of the universe has that energy and consciousness. Sadly, discussions of infinite possibility are often surrounded by skepticism and disbelief. However, such cynicism is often misidentified and misapplied because it tends to be based on the erroneous presupposition that infinite possibility is somehow abnormal and not truly viable or feasible.

Don't Live as the Effect of Life

In truth, infinite possibilities are all around us, waiting to be discovered. It is fundamental to recognize that energy and information exist everywhere in nature. People who have adopted the conventional business-as-usual mindset tend to set their aspirations and goals to what they have already judged to be possible according to contextual reality. They create their business from what they *believe in* rather than what they are *aware of.* Sorry to say, in an even more limiting way, they also confine themselves to what they think other people will pass judgment on as normal. They don't want to be ridiculed for being different. They don't want to be seen as not fitting in.

While the idea of leading from the edge of infinite possibility may seem illogical or impossible, please recognize that just because something appears impossible does not prove it to be illusory or erroneous. It just challenges our concept of what is possible. If we remain captivated by the code of contextual reality and the defensive attitude it fosters, the idea of leading from the edge of infinite possibility seems impossible and unconventional.

Can you imagine what your business and your life would be like if you could lead from the edge of infinite possibility? Would you be willing to acknowledge that so-called normal perceptions are flawed and misleading, because in contextual reality, you are only capable of sensing a fraction of energy from a minuscule portion of reality? Only when you are willing and able to recognize the limitation of your perception can you confront your assumptions and discover other possibility.

Discover the Secret

Have you ever wondered what sets certain remarkable business leaders apart from the rest? They seem to achieve things with ease and effortlessness. What makes it possible for them to prosper and thrive while the rest of us watch in awe and wonder? People who lead from the edge of infinite possibility recognize that the universe is an infinite place that has no boundaries or limitations. They choose to perceive everything, know everything, and be everything, which allows them to receive everything. They know that the universe will provide infinitely if they ask and are willing to receive. Those people who stand out as truly remarkable leaders, who have palpable presence, have already discovered the secret of leading from the edge of infinite possibility. They have claimed, owned, acknowledged, and embraced this intrinsic inner resource. These remarkable leaders live in the world as the greatness they are. They do everything from the place of consciousness that invites everybody else to be the greatness of them. That's the basis of leading from the edge of infinite possibility. It's also the source of greatness.

We see these qualities in all of our heroes, the people we admire and have a high regard for: Warren Buffett, who saw a possibility for making the world a better place by consciously choosing what expanded every aspect of this world and not just what worked for him. Steve Jobs, who was inspirational and provided visions that transformed the way people thought about what is possible, feasible, and attainable. Richard Branson, who exemplifies that true success is the ability to be driven by something grander than money. Muhammad Yunus, who turned begging bowls into cash boxes. Oprah Winfrey, who knows how to turn obstacles into new possibilities. Bill Strickland, who eradicates poverty through education and entrepreneurialism. Buckminster Fuller, who illustrates that all things are possible if we choose to question everything anew and refuse to believe there is anything that cannot be done. Martin Luther King, Jr., who saw the outrageous possibility of turning back centuries of hatred with dignity and nonviolence. Gary Douglas, who saw the possibility of generating a more conscious world through the use of simple tools that could be used by anyone. These conscious leaders and generative innovators demonstrate what it is like to lead and live from the edge of infinite possibility.

All of our heroes we mentioned above, well known or not, are compelling individuals who lead their lives and their businesses with conscious awareness. They have transcended limited circumstances and actualized infinite possibilities. They are not attached to convention or past reference points and they are always willing to take risks and destroy and un-create old systems, structures, and routines in favor of new ones. They live not as the effect of life, but as a contribution to it. They stand out from the crowd. What are the underlying common traits of these uncommon people who lead from the edge of infinite possibility?

- *They are aware of what is happening around them and they consciously choose whatever they do—or don't do. They are not attached to convention or past reference points. They are always willing to take risks.*

- *They create strategic innovation that generates change and transformation for their organization, their community, and the world. Because of their vision, awareness, consciousness, generosity of spirit, ingenuity, generative power, nonconformity, unconventionality, and creative talent, they are being a contribution. They generate substantial transformation in everyone who comes into contact with them. The technical skills they bring to an organization are much less important than the strategic awareness and prosperity consciousness they bring, as consciousness affects all people who come into contact with it.*

- *They live not as the effect of life, but as the source of it. They stand out from the crowd because they operate with non-contextual awareness at the same time they are functional within contextual reality.*

- *They have an awareness of what they would like to generate in the world energetically and they carry the awareness of that energy with them no matter where they go and what they do.*

- *They have the ability to be themselves, regardless of what occurs around them.*

- *They break new ground by bringing their consciousness to bear on their offerings, product, and services. They are conscious and aware in the way they express their vision, values, and strategies.*

Walk the Talk

As a leader of an organization, any time there is a gap between what you say and what you do, your trustworthiness will be questioned. People are always more inclined to follow a leader who walks the talk. If your organization is to thrive and provide real value, you as the leader, must choose to be conscious and aware in the way you express your vision, values, and strategies. If you want your employees and stakeholders to operate in a conscious way, with awareness, then you must walk the talk. How do you walk the talk? Are you being a conscious leader in your own life? You can create policies and procedures, issue standards of practice, and present all the inspirational speeches you want. If your employees and stakeholders don't see you being a conscious leader who endeavors to lead with conscious awareness every single day, they won't either.

Whenever we work with chief executives and boards, we stress the fact that they are the ones who have to choose to be conscious leaders. They have to be the first to expand their zone of awareness and stop functioning from the linear construct of reality. They cannot expect their employees to operate from the edge of infinite possibility if they are not willing to do it themselves. Most employees are boss-scrutinizers. People always take their cues from the chief executive and the leadership team of an organization.

It all comes down to the choices you make. Everything is choice. Everything is infinite possibility. You have consciousness. You are consciousness. You have a choice to be consciousness. If claimed, owned, and embraced wholeheartedly and sincerely, consciousness allows you to revel in your own greatness and extraordinariness without a sense of superiority or the need for hierarchy—and to inspire your team to do the same.

- *Are you choosing to lead from the edge of infinite possibility?*

- *Are you choosing to be a conscious leader?*

- *What are the obstacles that stand in the way of you choosing to become a conscious leader?*

- *What would need to change for you to choose to be a conscious leader?*

- *Do you have any idea of what it would be like to lead your business moment-by-moment as the conscious leader you truly are?*

- *Are you be willing to see that there may be a way to generate something totally different in your business if you are willing to change the way you view things?*

Be Willing to Be More in Every Respect

Leading from the edge of infinite possibility seems to come naturally to Bill Strickland, the CEO of Manchester Bidwell Corporation (MBC). We had the pleasure of meeting Bill when we presented at the Consciousness in Business conference in Santa Fe, New Mexico. As we listened to Bill talk about his projects and the way he created his organization, we were moved to see such a dramatic example of leading from the edge of infinite possibility. Bill Strickland's transformation from an at-risk youth to a recipient of the 1996 MacArthur Genius grant would be remarkable in itself, if it were not surpassed by the staggering breadth of his strategic awareness, vision, and ability to lead from the edge of infinite possibility.

At every turn, Manchester Bidwell Corporation has taken the road less traveled. Bill Strickland turned a near bankrupt community training center in Pittsburgh into one of the most successful organizations in America. For nearly three decades, he has worked to reinvent new approaches to social entrepreneurship and create a model for turning people with dead-end lives into productive members of society. In the Manchester neighborhood of Pittsburgh's North Side, Bill has forged a series of programs to bring new life to the community. Hearing his story and seeing what he has achieved left us convinced that everyone is capable of bringing real and remarkable changes to our world. His story can be read in his book, *Make the Impossible Possible: One Man's Crusade to Inspire Others to Dream Bigger and Achieve the Extraordinary.*

Bill Strickland's achievements, although seemingly miraculous, are not rare or unusual. In fact, it is possible for all of us to achieve extraordinary things if we choose to be the greatness we truly are. All things are possible if we are willing to step up and become more than what we have been willing to be in the past. This requires the willingness to be more in every respect.

Follow the Energy

Contrary to what many people think, leading from the edge of infinite possibility is not about controlling things. It's not about getting everything we want when we want it. And it's not about using force and effort to make things occur in our life. What most people create is based on the amount of energy they put into controlling things. Can you imagine how much energy is required of them as they attempt to control everything in order to make their business successful? Enormous amounts!

Leading from the edge of infinite possibility is about following energy rather than using force and effort as a way of making things occur in our life. Following the energy is about being willing to receive the information that is available. It is about being open to what the universe is sharing with us. It involves asking questions so that the universe has an avenue for responding. The universe is an unlimited place with unlimited possibilities. It will provide unlimited opportunities and possibilities if we ask it questions.

Life in the Pittsburgh neighborhood of Manchester, as most people experience it, involves a lot of hard work, a lot of effort, a lot of trauma, drama, upset, and intrigue—and not much joy. Yet Bill was able to see other possibilities because he didn't buy into erroneous beliefs about insufficiency that were based on the appearance of poverty. He did not accept current realities and instead chose to perceive beyond them. He asked questions, followed the energy, and made conscious choices based on the information and awareness he perceived and received.

You start with the perception that the world is an unlimited opportunity....
Then the question becomes, How are we going to rebuild the planet?
~ Bill Strickland

With only $122 in his bank account, Bill embarked upon a campaign to raise matching funds for a $250,000 National Endowment for the Arts grant. In 1986, following a successful capital campaign, he opened the $6.5 million Manchester Bidwell facility. Designed by a pupil of Frank Lloyd Wright, the 62,000-square-foot, honey-colored brick building houses Strickland's vision of a thriving community-learning center. The center currently provides training in fields as varied as gourmet food preparation: chemical, office, and medical technologies: and education arts programming in ceramics, photography, and digital imaging. In addition, the center presents nationally acclaimed jazz performances, and has its own jazz recording label, which has produced four Grammy-winning CDs. Each day, struggling high school and adult-vocational students enter a beautiful building of arches and circles designed to allow the sun to pour through.

The worst thing about being poor is what it does to your spirit, not just your wallet. I wanted to build something that would give the people who come here a vision of what life could be, to create an environment that says that life is good.
~ Bill Strickland

More than 90 percent of the high-risk high-school kids who have gone to Bill's Manchester Bidwell program have gotten their high school diploma, and 85 percent of them have gone on to college or some other form of higher education. More than 80 percent of the adults who have graduated from his vocational program have found jobs after graduation.

Manchester Bidwell has not succeeded simply as just a jobs training center and community arts program. It has actually transformed the lives of people on a fast-track to failure, brought new life to one of Pittsburgh's communities, and created a framework for turning people with dead-end lives into productive people. Bill's incredible achievement is not that he is dealing in enormous numbers, although his combined programs reach about 400 kids and 475 adults each year, but that Bill Strickland is dealing in real life transformational achievement. He helps people open their eyes and see the possibilities before them.

Things happen because I refused to be limited by what conventional wisdom, or other people, or the cautious little voice we all have in our heads told me I couldn't do. I haven't accomplished everything I set out to do, but I've accomplished a whole lot more than I would have if I'd let myself be boxed in by common sense and sensible expectations. I left the door open to possibility and, more often than not, opportunity showed its face. They gave me a Genius Award for thinking like that, but it's nothing any clear-thinking person can't manage. Each one of us, no matter who our parents are, where we live, how much education we have, or what kinds of connections, abilities, and opportunities life may have offered us, has the potential to shape our lives in ways that will bring us the success we long for.
~ Bill Strickland

Essential Insights

What makes Bill Strickland so noteworthy is that he has created an amalgamation of social activism and capitalism that has become a new framework and example for corporate community philanthropic partnerships. What can we learn from Bill Strickland's experience?

Step beyond the conventional business-as-usual paradigm.

There are no limits to what we can create.

Be willing to be, do, have, create, and generate everything in life.

Live in a constant state of creation of your life and business.

Choice and infinite possibility are real.

The edge of infinite possibility is intensity of awareness. In this space we have unlimited possibility, we are unhindered by the concern for competition and survival, and we are free from unconscious assumptions of the scarcity paradigm.

Leading from the edge of infinite possibility doesn't happen by itself. It is not a random event. In order to lead from the edge of infinite possibility, you have to stop functioning from the linear construct of this reality. Nothing has to change in your external environment or in the situation that surrounds you, for you to begin functioning from the edge of infinite possibility. You simply have to move into the space of non-contextual awareness.

CHAPTER SIX

The Intensity Of Non-Contextual Awareness

What if what is possible is much greater than anything anyone has
ever been able to see?
What if you could show business leaders what it was like to live
beyond this reality?
What choices could they have?
~ Gary Douglas

Non-contextual awareness is a natural gift and an intrinsic skill that we all have. It has been described as the ability to know without the use of rational thought processes or direct cognition. It is the capacity to know without words and to perceive the truth without explanation, cognitive interpretation, reasoning, or justification. Non-contextual awareness is, simply put, knowing that you know without knowing how you know. Society-changing individuals like Albert Einstein, Michelangelo, and Leonardo Da Vinci had an intensity of non-contextual awareness, and were thus able to tap into ideas from outside of time and space.

> *The intellect has little to do with the road to discovery. There comes a leap in consciousness, call it intuition or what you will, and the solution comes to you. You don't know how or why.*
> ~ *Albert Einstein*

Non-contextual awareness is the key to perceiving and receiving unlimited possibilities and seizing new opportunities. Your awareness is amazingly more vast and unlimited than anything your mind can comprehend or create, and its possibilities are boundless. So, why would you settle with using your mind to create your reality in the limited way you have been? Why would you choose to operate in a way that limits what is possible for you and your business?

Choose to Be Non-Contextual Awareness

In our view, if you wish to make your business take off from wherever it is right now, you must nurture your non-contextual awareness. Analysis alone will never be adequate. Most people doubt their awareness and rely solely on empirical evidence as the basis for their decision-making processes. We believe that empirical evidence is useful—but only in a limited way. It is designed to ensure one's survival. It is about continued existence. Relying on empirical evidence may keep you in business, but at the same time, it won't allow you to operate on the edge of what is possible. In short, it keeps you from thriving and flourishing.

If this is the case, why do so many business leaders choose to remain anchored in contextual reality? The answer is that the idea of non-contextual awareness frightens the average business executive for two reasons. First, because the conventional business paradigm treats non-contextual awareness as an extraordinary quality exclusively restricted for geniuses, whiz kids, and the elite few. This conveniently offers a handy reason and justification to preserve and safeguard the conventional business-as-usual way of doing things. Second, because it seems somehow "soft" and at odds with the forceful and hard-hitting tactics deemed essential to succeed in the business jungle.

The truth of the matter is just the opposite. Recent studies by the Shell Oil Company and Harvard researchers have confirmed that top executives frequently attribute up to 80 percent of their success to insight. They discovered that high levels of instinctive insight are often found in the top tiers of organizations. Being aware does not make these executives superior to others; it simply makes them more conscious and more open to what is possible. Ask successful and well-known business leaders how they achieved such remarkable success, and they will tell you it involved awareness and trusting their inner knowing. Awareness is commonly known as instinct, intuition, gut feeling, or insight. Many of the world's top movers and shakers are attuned to their awareness and use it to propel their businesses forward. Here are just a few examples:

- *Oprah Winfrey, the world-famous talk show host, says it was her awareness, insight, and instinct that led her from a news anchor job in Baltimore to hosting her own talk show in Chicago and on to her phenomenal career as an internationally renowned TV personality and philanthropist. Oprah said: "Follow your instincts. That's where true wisdom manifests itself."*

- *Warren Bennis, distinguished professor and management guru, calls awareness his "inner voice." He believes that listening to it and trusting it is one of the most important skills of leadership that he has learned. In his view, successful people from all walks of life rely as much on their awareness and abstract skills as on their logical and analytical talent.*

- *Dr. Jonas Salk, the renowned virologist who discovered the first vaccine against poliomyelitis stated, "It is always with excitement that I wake up in the morning wondering what my awareness will toss up to me, like gifts from the sea. I work with it and rely on it. It's my partner."*

- *Michael Munn, Ph.D., a former aerospace chief scientist for Lockheed and an award-winning engineer, stated that as he and his team worked on the cutting edge of science where there was no one to follow, they deliberately took timeouts to meditate and access their inner knowing and intuition. Munn said, "How do I know the answers are there? I see pictures or movies or dreamlike sequences. I have an immediate inner knowing that this is the revelation for which I was waiting. My awareness lets me know, 'This is it'!"*

Non-Contextual Awareness Precedes Cognition

Non-contextual awareness is not a magical sixth sense or a paranormal process. Neuroscientist Joseph LeDoux has identified the amygdala as the site in the brain that relates to non-contextual awareness and insight. The amygdala distinguishes stimuli and triggers behavior faster than cognitive processes. LeDoux has shown that non-contextual awareness precedes cognition, logic, and analytical process. Awareness, in short, is the source from which innovation, creativity, and new products and services will flow. Innovation and creativity depend largely on how you personally connect with your awareness.

Contribute to Things in a Different Way

Non-contextual awareness is about possibilities, choices, and awareness. When you generate from this space, you have no investment in the outcome—and no idea of what might show up. There is only awareness of the energy. When you start to function from non-contextual awareness, you'll begin to see that you have an energy that you can contribute to things in a different way than you may have thought possible. A great example of this is the work of Sir Timothy John Berners-Lee, the British inventor of the World Wide Web.

The World Wide Web started life in the CERN physics laboratory in Switzerland in the early 1990s. Berners-Lee introduced the Internet to the world in a paper called "Information Management: A Proposal," in which he married up hypertext with the Internet to create a system for sharing and distributing information, not just within a company, but globally. What makes the Web all the more remarkable is that even though Tim Berners-Lee first developed it as an academic tool to allow scientists to share data, he perceived and received the infinite potential and possibility of the Internet beyond anyone's imagination—and it has since developed in unconceivable directions throughout the entire world. He also created the first Web browser and editor. The world's first website, http://info.cern.ch (still in existence), was launched in 1991. It explained the World Wide Web concept and gave users an introduction to getting started with their own websites. The Web is now the ever-present network via which information is shared globally on the Internet. An estimated 165 million websites now exist, the BBC recently reported.

At the same time that Tim Berners-Lee introduced the World Wide Web to the world freely, competing technologies, such as Gopher, developed at the University of Minnesota in the United States, were also offering a way of connecting documents on the Internet for a price. But the World Wide Web succeeded because Tim Berners-Lee knew that for the Web to reach its full potential, it would have to be freely available. He set strategy for the Internet based on the concept of network neutrality, where everyone has the same level of access to the Web and all data moving around the Web is treated equally. He perceived that the Web had infinite potential to develop in unimaginable directions, but above all, he had it in mind that it should be a force for good.

One the most essential things about the Web is that with a click you can go any place. There is not a French Web or an English Web; they are linked not separate. The Web is not divided into good and low quality documents; it is not divided between academic and commercial, there is no discrimination, it is just one Web, free and open for all and that's its power.
~ Tim Berners-Lee, February 2009

Not all the bosses at CERN were in favor of making the Web universally accessible. Since the world knew nothing about the potential of the Web, most conventional strategic analysis would have pointed to limited potential for growth. Tim Berners-Lee had to convince them that the Web was such an immense innovation that CERN couldn't hold on to it, and the best thing to do was to give it away. He persuaded his bosses to provide the program code for free. Since then, the Web has exploded into every area of life. According to recent figures offered by Internet World Stats, there are an estimated 1.133 billion people around the world engaging in regular use of the Internet. And with more than 165 million different destinations available through its virtual pages, the Internet has grown into a groundbreaking, and seemingly limitless, communications tool.

Apart from his pioneering idea, what makes Tim Berners-Lee extraordinarily special is his amazing generosity of spirit, the fact that he gave his invention away freely, with no patents or royalties. He has, however, since become exceptionally wealthy. We believe this is because he has chosen to create his life and his business from how much consciousness he can create and what contribution he can be instead of how much money he could make.

Cultivate Non-Contextual Awareness

Non-contextual awareness is a real psycho-physiological experience that each of us can choose to have right now. This is the realm of infinite possibility. The fact is non-contextual awareness is our innate aptitude, like intelligence and eye-hand coordination. It can be strengthened and enhanced through training and practice. However, our modern cultural bias for intellect and analysis doesn't value awareness as highly as it should.

Most of us have experienced moments of intensity of non-contextual awareness, when we were "in the zone" or "in the flow." In this space, we are lucid and coherent, and things are in harmony and in sync. There is a heightened awareness and sensitivity. Our actions and purposes are matched, and the outcomes are dynamic, creative, efficient, and rewarding. Nothing seems impossible. We feel connected to something greater than our immediate task. To expand your non-contextual awareness requires you to come out of any limited points of view you might have created. If you wish to expand your non-contextual awareness you have to be willing to receive everything. You also have to be willing to perceive, know, and be everything in life.

Receiving *is the ability to be in allowance of everything and everyone as they are—without judgment, without resisting and reacting, or aligning and agreeing. It is about remaining constantly open, vulnerable,* and unresisting to any energy. The willingness to receive means you recognize that all things can come to you, and they don't stick with you. They keep on going. For example, if you are unwilling to receive being judged by other people, you may become overly concerned with other people's points of view. You may become overly concerned with what people think of you. When you are unwilling to receive, you contract and withdraw your non-contextual awareness, and whatever you can't receive becomes a limitation to your awareness.

Perceiving is about being aware of the energy of the energy in everyone and everything, at all times. If you are willing to perceive the energy in all aspects of your life, your life expands. Perception is like the wind. The wind doesn't solidify and become a truth or non-truth; it just is. It keeps moving and changing and it is never the same, one moment to the next. If you are willing to have the perception of all things, then you are aware of the energy flows.

Knowing is the intelligent flow of insight that transpires instantaneously once the mind and emotions are balanced, calm, and coherent. It is a dimension of consciousness far deeper than thoughts and feelings. Knowing is awareness of what is possible without having any judgment about it. When you follow your knowing, you are aware whether your choice will be expansive and create more possibilities or contractive and create limitation for you and everyone else. Functioning from knowing is not done through force and exertion. It occurs by following the energy, which is about asking questions so that the universe and your inner knowing have an avenue for responding.

Being is about relating to life in spontaneous interaction with the energy of the moment, without thought, without intention, without desire or consideration of the next moment. You cannot receive if you cannot be. All the limitations in your life about what you think you can't receive are based on what you are unwilling to be.

We have found that when business leaders choose to expand their non-contextual awareness, they also expand their potency and influence as leaders. When they function from perceiving, knowing, being, and receiving, they are not easily misled by shallow analyses, misinformed by superficial information or swindled by deception. When leaders live and function from total perceiving, knowing, being, and receiving, they expand their capacity to achieve outstanding short-term results while taking matters into consideration from a long-term perspective.

Reflection

Do you figure that if you can't explain something, it's not truly possible?

Have you decided you can't know anything beyond what is cognitive?

Have you misidentified and misapplied cognitive capacity as awareness?

These are important questions. You are unlikely to expand your non-contextual awareness if you have mistaken cognitive capacity as awareness. In a sense, mistaking cognitive capacity for awareness is a zero-sum situation: The more fixed and adamant you are about your beliefs and the more constricting the shackles of your mental model regarding cognitive capacity are, the less likely you are to expand your non-contextual awareness.

The Value of Asking Questions

Sometimes the real hurdle to prosperity and success is not a lack of options, but a lack of ability to perceive the infinite possibilities that are available. The culprit? Our upbringing and cultural indoctrination that foster cognitive ability, judgment, rationality, conventionality, and conformity yet place little value on awareness, originality, audacity, and eccentricity. To put it simply, most of us are taught to come to conclusion instead of functioning from awareness and asking what the possibilities are. We tend to be so fixed and adamant about what we already know and believe to be true that we limit ourselves to the things that we know. The result: We are often unable to see what is truly possible. When you try to work out the right answer, you go into your mind. You reach conclusions that are based on what you already know. And once you have an answer, that's the sum total of what can show up for you.

Every time you ask a question and expect to find the right answer, you eliminate the awareness of the infinite possibilities you actually have. An answer is always about how to get it right. A right answer eliminates other possibilities from your reality and life. Every answer is the eradication of your awareness, because as soon as you think you have the answer, you won't allow yourself to have the awareness of what else is possible.

What Is Living in the Question?

Living in the question is not trying to get to the right answer or the right solution. It means using questions to bypass the limited answers your mind provides. Questions destabilize fixed points of view and shake the mind loose from its presumptions. They impel your mind beyond the rut of timeworn blueprints. Unlimited questions are far more valuable than the so-called right answers because they open the door to all possibility.

Living in the question is the practice of inviting the universe to support you by asking unlimited questions. When you ask a nonlinear and unlimited question and you don't have a preconceived idea of an expected outcome or answer, you set the stage for receiving insights otherwise unattainable.

Here are examples of what people often say to themselves when they deal with business issues and concerns: *This is so complicated I don't even know where to start. I can't get my head around the details! I don't know how to deal with this situation! My job is on the line if I can't fix this problem. I've got to figure it out! I don't know what to do about this problem! I am so worried; I can't possibly do this! etc. If leaders think "I can't do this", are they ever going to be able to do it? Instead of having these unproductive thoughts and being overwhelmed by problems, leaders can choose to ask the more conscious, nonlinear questions such as What is it I'm not getting about this?*

What am I pretending not to know or denying I know about this? What would it take for this to happen? What are the infinite possibilities that this will work out much better than we could ever imagine?

These questions are exceptional tools for how to know what is appropriate to do about the situation or the problem. When leaders ask these types of questions, things start to show up for them in a different way. The more leaders ask the question, the more aware leaders become of the options and possibilities they have. When asking the question, it is essential to avoid having expected outcomes. The key question is, "What are the infinite possibilities in this moment?" In this way, unlimited potential and infinite possibilities will emerge in ways that leaders may never have imagined possible. The question, How do we do this?" is not a real question. It is the answer we are looking for. Asking "how" is looking for answers, solutions, and conclusions to achieve a predetermined result. The questions must be asked with genuine wonder, not with attitude and certain expected outcomes. Stop seeking answers; instead put the focus on the questions themselves. If leaders ask the question in a nonlinear and unlimited way, and if they don't have a preconceived idea and expected outcome about the answer, they set the stage for previously unthinkable leaps of consciousness. If leaders open up to genuine wonder, they step out of the zone of this reality and into that of infinite possibilities.

Albert Einstein is a great example of someone who lived in the question. His willingness to perceive, know, be, and receive the energies of the universe was his ticket to total awareness. It gave him information about what was possible, and he was able to access universal knowledge. He questioned the whole notion of time, proposing that speed would allow us to travel beyond the present. He refused to be constrained by the finite potential of contextual reality. His work and achievements did not come from his cognitive ability, but from living in the question. This is where the magic begins.

The most beautiful experience we can have is the mysterious. It is the fundamental emotion that stands at the cradle of true art and true science.
~ Albert Einstein

Possibility, Choice, Question and Contribution

The questions you can ask are innumerable. But remember, they must be unlimited questions, which will open you to the infinite possibilities—and not questions in search of an answer. A good place to begin developing the practice of living in the question is with the process of Possibility, Choice, Question, and Contribution. This process—and these questions—have wide-ranging applicability in all areas of your life. You ask the question, and the universe will provide you with an awareness of what is possible.

Here are the key questions to use:

- *What's possible here?*

- *What choice do I have here?*

- *What question is there that will expand my life?*

- *What contribution can I be?*

Here are some examples of the way these questions could have been used by the executives at Kodak to deal with the threat posed by the digital revolution, avert the demise of their film business, and discover powerful new opportunities. How could you use them in your business?

What's possible here?
When the executives at Kodak first perceived the emergence of digital photography more than twenty-five years ago, if they had chosen to ask, "What's possible here?" they wouldn't have ignored this threat. They would have perceived how digital photography might impact their business and investigated different possibilities.

What choices do we have here?
If they asked themselves, "What choices do we have here?" they could have taken advantage of the early warnings and prepared for the digital

world. They could have secured a greater share of sales of cameras and printers and possibly the revenue from Internet photo sites and cell phone cameras. They most likely would have considered all their options instead of assuming that the business would continue as it had for decades. They would have focused on trying to do the same things better. They would not have committed themselves to what was not working, and they would not have continued to operate from the same limited set of options.

What question is there that will expand our business?

If Kodak's executives had asked, "What question is there that will expand our business?" they would have been able to ask many more questions like:

> *What can we do differently that would generate different possibilities?*
>
> *What needs to change?*
>
> *What are the possibilities that the electronic system will be low enough in price to have widespread appeal?*

These questions would have allowed them to perceive the flaws and drawbacks of their strategy more clearly and quickly. They might have recognized that traditional film and prints could become obsolete if in-home, personal electronic systems became comparable in terms of price and quality with commercial printing services. If Kodak's leadership had chosen to ask "What question is there that will expand our business?" they would never have maintained their fixed point of view that the future would be just a variant of the present. They would have recognized that it was time to shift strategic direction. At that point, they could have asked:

Is it possible that the digital revolution could radically wipe out our whole market?

What do we have to do differently?

What is this is going to look like?

Will things go in the direction we think they should?

These questions would have freed them to generate different possibilities.

What contribution can we be?

Kodak would not have lost 75 percent of its stock market value if its leaders had asked, "What contribution can we be?" They would have seen the contribution they could be in the in the emerging digital world. When leaders are being a contribution, they always have choice. They are able to make decisions efficiently, quickly, strategically, and with conscious awareness. They have the awareness to know what is or could be happening and where they are going.

Some Additional Questions You Can Ask

- *What else can I be doing?*

- *What else is possible?*

- *What else can I learn about?*

- *What else can I discover?*

- *What else can I perceive?*

- *What else can I do?*

- *What else is there?*

- *What question could I ask that would expand my life?*

    Behind every conscious leader is a long string of questions.

Mastering the Art of Living in the Question

Perhaps the best way to convey the intricacy of the potency of living in the question is through an anecdote from our own work. We are often called in by boards to help them work through dysfunctional aspects of their governance or to raise their levels of awareness so that they can have an even greater impact. A few years ago we received a call from the CEO of a major mental health institute requesting help in creating greater strategic awareness in their board.

From the moment we met with the board, we saw that their culture was out of sync with what they needed to generate and bring about. The board saw themselves as the source and believed everything began and ended with them. They were the answer to everything. Functioning from being the source of the organization required the board to constantly judge whether they had it "right." They were in a constant state of measuring themselves against others because, as the source, they could not allow anyone else to contribute to them. They had fallen into an organizational rut and were incapable of shifting strategy and tactics as the situation warranted. The board did not function well with the course of change, but instead tried to hang onto their security and resisted what they did not understand.

From our first meeting with the board, we had to deal with the resistance, opposition, and fixed mindsets of some board members. We were aware that our effectiveness depended on our ability to live in the question and be in allowance of people who were not willing to change. Fortunately, the board chair and a few board members recognized that if the organization was going to thrive, the organizational practices and the culture of the board had to change. However, some of the old guard were set in their ways and unwilling to receive this view. They kept saying, "It ain't broke, so why fix it?"

We have learned over time that we cannot force people to change or receive and adapt to new possibilities if they do not want to. Change and transformation cannot be generated from control, force, and effort. Forcing change would have been met with strong resistance from disgruntled board members. Instead we had to invite the board to look at a different possibility. We were not there to change their minds. We were there to open their awareness to what they had been choosing and how their choices were creating their business. We hoped they would see that they had the option of changing things.

We began the process of working with them by employing the practice of living in the question. We asked the universe and ourselves:

What do we need to be aware of here?

What can be changed with this board to allow them to raise their levels of awareness so they can have a greater impact on the community they serve?

What generative energy, space, and consciousness can we be that will facilitate a change here?

What contribution can we be?

These questions moved things in a generative direction. We allowed ourselves to have the awareness of what came up when we asked the questions, and then we started following the energy of what was going to create and generate more space for this board.

We became aware that the biggest untapped possibility for their business success was changing the way board members and the executive leadership team worked together to govern and lead the business.

Their way of working together created limitations and was, to a large extent, the source of problems in their organization. We invited the board members and leadership team to meet together in an open forum to resolve apprehension and potential conflicts. The session started with the questions:

What points of view and systems govern and control your organization?

Are they working well for the organization?

What needs to change?

What can be done about it?

These questions brought issues into the open and ensured no anti-conscious schemes were being created to sabotage the project. We noticed that a few leaders and board members kept looking for the rightness or wrongness of things in order to find a reason to make changes.

To help overcome their reluctance to perceiving different possibilities, we became the catalyst and the stimulus to change by patiently and steadily being the question that allowed them to look at themselves differently. We asked questions about what occurred and what they perceived should have occurred, and we then asked more questions that brought them to a new awareness. We wished to give them an opportunity to see that they had other choices, so we asked them to consider:

What have you been unwilling or unable to change in your business that you would actually like to change?

What does the business require?

What do your clients and stakeholders require?

Would they be willing to actually have change?

We made sure that we did not take sides or align and agree with any point of view. When we didn't try to make our point of view right and others' points of view wrong, it allowed people to change their story, because they no longer had to defend the rightness of their point of view. And since we had no judgment of anything, we created a space for them to look at everything for what it was—not what they wanted it to be, not what they thought it ought to be, and not what we thought it should be—but just for what it was. When people felt that they could be themselves and that they weren't being judged, they were able to step back from their fixed positions and allow other ideas and possibilities to be present in their awareness.

We asked questions that empowered them to see what they could already be, what they already knew, what they could already receive, and what they were refusing to be, know, perceive, and receive. As we asked more questions, we generated more clarity in their universe about the background story that predicated this meeting in the first place. They gained insight into who they were being as the leaders of the organization. The questions allowed them to see what they were doing, so that they might have a different choice available.

Bringing conflicts to the surface and having a conversation with the board members and leadership team in an atmosphere of no judgment—just allowance and observation—allowed the team to perceive what their points of view were, which gave them awareness of where they were functioning from. They were able to acknowledge that their fixed points of view were creating the way their business was showing up. They were able to perceive and receive that control was an illusion, and that the obsessive pursuit of control established limitation, restriction, and constraints in the organization. They also recognized that any time they judged something or came to a conclusion about it; they didn't allow anything that didn't match it to come into their awareness.

By being the question instead of being the answer, we were able to facilitate their awareness of what their points of view were all about. We pointed out that they had a different choice and a different possibility and we invited them to let go of their fixed points of view, to change them, or to have more insight about the viewpoints they had been functioning from. Eventually all the leaders saw merit in what we were doing and chose to get on with the job of leading the organization strategically with awareness.

In this meeting, the board and leadership saw that they had inadvertently followed a governance model that required them to sustain a controlled structure in which staff follow specified directives and performed them efficiently and in a best-practice manner. They became aware that this conventional model was not working for them and decided they would like to change it.

We invited them to initiate the practice of living in the question and to take stock of their current internal condition by asking:

- *What else is possible?*

- *What choices do we have here?*

- *What question will expand our business?*

- *What contribution can we be?*

- *What can we do differently that will create a different result?*

Their willingness to look at what else they could create and what would create different possibilities kept them in the forward motion of generating and renewing their organization. This fostered real insight and inspiration, which allowed them to generate something totally different in their organization.

The more the board and leadership team experienced the phenomenon of living in the question, the more intrigued they became. The more they asked questions, the more aware they became of the options and possibilities they had. They became aware that they could change anything by living in the question. All of the sudden, a light went on! Instead of coming up with a particular solution that was based on past conceptions, they became aware of different possibilities. They started to truly be strategic, rather than simply following a strategic plan that was outdated the day it was approved. They built the practice of asking questions into their board meetings, expected the staff reports and proposals to address these questions, and started to really get what it was like to function from possibility and choice. As a direct result of this, they were able to move into new fields relating to mental health, attract a new breed of directors who also were interested in making a contribution to stakeholders and society generally, and to create significant new revenue streams.

The beauty of the living in the question is that it can be applied to all kinds of situations and circumstances. Leaders can employ this practice to solve problems, develop ideas, and generate new and different possibilities. The power of the practice lies in its simplicity. Questions give business leaders the opportunity to see that there are different ways of looking at the world and to know that there is a way to generate totally different possibilities in their organization. As unique a practice as it is, living in the question reflects a universally shared conscious leadership mindset. It is a profound skill to be mastered.

Expanding Your Non-Contextual Awareness

The speed, complexity, and unpredictable nature of change in the global business environment can make us baffled and overwhelmed. These external changes are massive, sudden, rapid, and full of contradictory signals. Leaders need to expand the bandwidth of their non-contextual awareness in order to simultaneously perceive and receive situations from multiple perspectives, from the big picture to the small details.

As change speeds up, investing in non-contextual awareness is no longer just a good idea; it's now an essential business strategy. Rapid changes in the business arena cause much uncertainty and put a high premium on spotting or creating changes in the market before others do. Leaders with well-developed non-contextual awareness deal with change, complexity, and chaos more effectively than those who are less conscious. They are able to perceive what is going on around them and take action quickly. In contrast, leaders who subscribe to the conventional business-as-usual paradigm tend to be myopic. They focus on the business close at hand. They tend to have deadly blind spots and miss opportunities.

Leaders must develop and expand non-contextual awareness so they can be ready for high-velocity business, keep their perceptual lenses open to receive essential information, and avoid relying too much on the past for indications of what might happen in the future. They also need to be aware of the globalization of consumer lifestyles and comprehend what that means to their organization. Ask yourself:

How well do I understand the new hyper-change world?

How aware am I of globalization of consumer lifestyles?

Do I comprehend what these really mean to my organization?

Perceive and Receive the Change That Is Happening

The major radical trends that will change the business landscape are the coming global and social innovation economy, hyper-innovation, sophisticated technologies, integrated supply chains, real-time dynamic information, immense global collaboration, geopolitics, climate change, environmental footprints, executive derailment, off-shoring, and disappearing barriers to entry. They change the game of business. Dealing with these changes requires nimbleness, redefining paradigms, and the willingness to look at all possibilities. In other words, it requires non-contextual awareness.

Failure to recognize trends or opportunities beyond an organization's primary area of business results in missed opportunities. But leaders who have superior non-contextual awareness, see opportunities sooner and gain a profitable advantage over their blinkered counterparts. For example, Apple, with the iPod phenomena, changed the way people listen to music, Google shook up the media industry, and Skype disrupted the telecommunications industry.

To thrive as a business innovator in today's environment, you need to be open to playing an entirely new game. You need to break out of conventional models that dictate how you are supposed to function. You must destroy and un-create the old business boundaries that define how you operate. Are you aware of your persistent blind spots? What are the different possibilities and opportunities that may be right in front of you that you are refusing to see?

Generative Exploration

For those who wish to make a connection with what it would take to perceive and receive the change that is happening, a simple technique called Generative Exploration can help. Here's how it works. Look at your current situation and ask these empowering questions:

- *What is happening currently?*

- *Could a current situation be changed or done differently?*

- *What can I do about it?*

- *What else is possible?*

- *What possibilities exist that I haven't thought of yet?*

- *What if everything that was possible in the world was available at our request?*

Don't expect an immediate answer to your questions. An awareness of what might be may show up somewhat later. It rarely shows up immediately. Simply continue asking these questions and allow yourself to receive new insights and awareness. Empowering questions generate the space and conditions that foster openness and release stuck energy. New possibilities emerge, not from the right answer or opinion, but from the free movement of awareness.

Whenever you recognize that something isn't working, ask: "What can I do differently that would work—at least for me?": not "How do I fix it?" The target of this practice is not to find the right answer, but to perceive things from different perspectives.

In doing this exercise, cultivate the mindset that there is no such thing as the correct answer. When you look for the answer, you're looking for it based on what you already know, what you've judged, or what you've decided can be the answer. Every answer is the eradication of your awareness, because as soon as you believe you have the answer or think you have it right, you won't allow yourself to have the awareness of what else is possible.

There are infinite numbers of what appear to be answers—but none of them are *the* answer. Awareness about something can take many different paths. Try asking:

> *Okay, what's this going to look like?*
>
> *Which of these alternatives is going to lead to the most expansion for me and everybody else?*
>
> *Will this choice be rewarding?*

Each question invites more awareness and more possibility. The point of asking questions is to gain different perspectives and be open to different possibilities. Living in the question can be a transformational practice. The discipline of living in the question allows you to perceive different possibilities in the most challenging situations and to receive in totality the abundance and exuberance of life. When you choose to live in the question you will be instantly transported into the realm of infinite possibilities.

> *The important thing is not to stop questioning. Curiosity has its own reason for existing.*
> *~ Albert Einstein*

The Essence of Generative Exploration

When asking questions, keep your awareness on the question, not on the million other thoughts, feelings, emotions, and worries you may have.

Be genuinely inquisitive and sincerely curious. Avoid desperately seeking the answer.

Question everything. Never come to a conclusion. Answer every question with another question.

Generative exploration frees you to practice expanding your non-contextual awareness so you can perceive what is going on around you and know how to take action quickly. You will be able to perceive different possibilities for creation and reinvention when others only see extinction or decline. You will be able to perceive and receive possibilities and risks before they become obvious to everyone else. You can be totally responsive and shift with each new set of circumstances. You will be able to perceive the major trends that will change the business landscape and draw on your awareness to make choices that will create greater future potential for your organization.

Embrace This Way of Being in Your Own Life

There are two practices required to bring non-contextual awareness into our daily life.

1. Question, Choice, Possibility, and Contribution.

Most of us have experienced non-contextual awareness. It's the experience where you were totally present and in the moment. You were able to take in a wide range of information and see things from a broader perspective. The question is: What is it going to take for this to become your modus operandi and state of being all the time? What if embracing this way of being is simply a matter of choice? It *is* merely a choice. Awareness shows up as a result of your choosing it. Being non-contextual awareness is about right here, right now. It occurs the moment you choose to be all that is possible. As very young children, we were frequently in non-contextual awareness. We marveled in the experience but we didn't understand it. As adult business leaders, we can use the four principles of Question, Choice, Possibility, and Contribution as conscious ways to expand our non-contextual awareness. The universe whispers secrets to conscious leaders when others hear only the random clatter.

So, what would it take for you to embrace this way of being in your own life and business?

2. Become aware of limited points of view.

To truly embody non-contextual awareness, you must come out of any limited points of view you have created. Your awareness is only limited by your refusing to perceive, know, be, and receive everything without any limitations, fixed points of view, or judgments. We know that the moment people take the initiative to become aware of their limitations, habits, and unconscious conditioning, they are on the path to unleashing and expanding their awareness.

Awareness resides within each of us as an infinite reservoir of intuitive knowing, wisdom, and acumen. If claimed, owned, and embraced wholeheartedly, it allows us to embrace our own extraordinariness and greatness. A famous quote from Michelangelo captures the notion of our intrinsic faculty and the need to strip away limiting detritus in order to bring that gift into the world: "Inside every block of stone or marble dwells a beautiful statue; one need only remove the excess material to reveal the work of art within."

Six things to do

Many people perceive deep inside that they do have this potential, but they do not know that it is possible to unleash and expand it. We know for certain that people can develop and expand their awareness because we have done it ourselves, and we have facilitated many leaders to do it as well. Can you imagine what it would be like if you could chip away at the marble, get rid of whatever concealed and obscured your awareness? The first step is to claim, own, and acknowledge that infinite awareness is already inside of you. To expand your zone of non-contextual awareness, you must:

1. Disidentify from the mind. You will not be able to expand your awareness as long as you are in your mind. You contract your awareness when you identify with your thoughts, feelings, and emotions; when you define yourself in a particular way; and when you try to "figure things out." Expanding awareness means rising above thoughts, feelings, and emotions. Every time you stop identifying with the mind, your zone of awareness expands.

2. Become willing to perceive, know, be, and receive everything without any limitations, fixed points of view, or judgments.

3. Give up having to have the answer and become willing to live in the question.

4. Give up defining yourself in any way, shape, or form. Come out of any limited points of view about yourself that you might have created

5. Become aware of the boundaries and restrictions that control and establish conventional practices and habitual behaviors—and then deliberately step beyond them.

6. Become the needlessness and to function as the infinite chaos.

A Matter of Discipline

When it comes to generating no-more-business-as-usual, a company's unconscious conditioning and legacy paradigm are a huge liability. The pursuit of non-contextual awareness must be the core to daily living, not a sideline activity or event. This kind of discipline requires a fundamental mind shift. It takes determination, sincerity, and commitment. Once you are able to consistently expand your non-contextual awareness, your next step is to unshackle yourself from the hypnotic power of contextual reality and to liberate your business from any unconscious conditioning.

In our experience, few organizations have a process for challenging their unconscious conditioning. Yet as you'll see in subsequent chapters, the ability to operate beyond contextual reality and to be functional with this contextual reality is the primary means for making organizations more generative, more innovative, and more successful.

Quick Tool

When you're in touch with everything, you have total awareness. Here is a quick tool to get you into the space to be aware of everything. Each morning, ask yourself:

What do I need to be aware of today?

Is there some place I need to put my energy or my attention today?

You can then direct whatever energy or attention is required to those areas, to keep things moving. That's having follow-through. You're in the question and following the energy. When you function from non-contextual awareness, there is no investment in the outcome and no idea of what might show up; there is only awareness of the energy. You are willing to receive all energies and no judgment is required.

Reflection

Are you alert to and aware of opportunity-maximizing and risk-minimizing strategies?

Do you have the ability to see the big picture as well as having total clarity about the details of a situation?

Do you have the broad of awareness bandwidth required to look far out onto the horizon, and comprehend the complexities of the external and global environment?

Do you have ability to detect patterns and determine what they mean for your business?

CHAPTER SEVEN

The Ultimate Freedom: Awareness and True Knowing

Knowing is awareness of what the possibilities are without having any judgment about them. In economic times like these, awareness opens doors to opportunities.
~ Gary Douglas

From childhood and adolescence to adulthood and old age, most people use limitation as a contrivance for knowledge. What we believe, think, do, and say begins as a cultural conditioning, then becomes a habit, and then stays on as our reality. Cultural conditioning is not just a state of mind; it's a form of conduct that directs everything we do. It can be self-sabotaging. And it's highly contagious.

The most limiting form of cultural conditioning is the way we take in new information and attempt to fit it into the context that already exists in our heads. We don't generally use the new information to question or challenge the soundness or truthfulness of what's already in there. We have been brainwashed to choose where we fit, where we benefit, where we win, and where we avoid losing. We attempt to maintain a relationship with everything in contextual reality rather than going beyond it. We create our life from what we *believe in* instead of what we are *aware of.*

For many centuries it was widely considered impossible for a human being to run a mile (1,609 meters) in under four minutes. In fact, many people believed that the four-minute mile was a physical barrier that no runner could break without causing significant damage to his or her health. An athlete named Roger Bannister was willing to ask, "What else is possible here?" On May 6, 1954, during an athletic meeting between the British AAA and Oxford University, Roger Bannister ran a mile in 3 minutes, 59.4 seconds—and broke through the four-minute mile psychological barrier. What made this event so noteworthy was that within three years, sixteen other runners also cracked the four-minute mile and broke through the previously impenetrable barrier. What happened to the belief regarding the physical barrier that prevented people from running the four-minute mile? This example shows that the belief was just an illusion based on contextual reality! When another possibility was documented as true, it changed the so-called reality of what was possible.

When you believe business structures are inflexible, business boundaries are defined, and you are forced to compete within them—that's cultural conditioning and brainwashing. You have been acculturated to believe that business is about competing, staying alive, winning, losing, and surviving in a world of scarcity and limited possibility. These beliefs may appear so ordinary and common as to disappear into the background of your day-to-day living. They are the "normal" ways of doing business. The fact of their acceptance as normal is the reason many organizations experience limited success and prosperity.

Leaders of organizations that subscribe to the conventional business-as-usual paradigm often engage in activities each day that, at a deep level, do not feel expansive or generative to them, but have become an accepted part of their everyday business practices and procedures. There is no real choice there.

Have courage to follow your heart and intuition. They somehow already know what you truly want to become. Everything else is secondary.
~ Steve Jobs, commencement address, Stanford University 2005

Hypnotized by Contextual Reality

Each of us has grown up in a family and society that had a particular point of view. No matter how objective we try to be, we continue to perceive the world through the context in which we were trained. We have been implanted with points of view that have taught us to function in the linearity of contextual reality. All our learning has been about how to be in context with it.

The truth of the matter is that we have been hypnotized by contextual reality to accept false points of view as if they were fact. We fabricate reasons and justifications for our behaviors, habits, and actions that are normal, reasonable, and plausible. These are guided by the assumptions we have made and the points of view we have been taught. When we accept without question something that is not true, it means that all of our points of view, actions, and reactions are based upon a false belief. For example, many people believe that to be a good leader, they have to sustain a controlled structure in which staff follow specified directives and perform them efficiently and in the approved manner. This view of leadership is power-based. It requires leaders to control their team and have power over them. If you subscribe to this point of view about leadership, you will seek to preserve the status quo and make good "soldiers" of the team. In our experience, this is a subtle misidentification and misapplication of the notion of leadership. While leaders can use their position to dictate and force staff to obey, it is important to recognize that it is just not possible to truly control other people. Why? Because people are unpredictable, uncontainable, uncontrollable, paradoxical, and unruly. They can be forced to obey, but they cannot be controlled in the traditional sense.

Limited by the Rightness of Your Point of View

Perhaps the biggest barrier to generating no-more-business-as-usual is believing in the rightness of your point of view. Every single point of view you have keeps you spellbound and limits your ability to have non-contextual awareness. You become mesmerized by your point of view. You are entrenched in its rightness. To entrench a point of view is to dig a particular path and decide it is the only way you can get to where you wish to be. It's all about *should, have to,* and *no choice.*

Deciding that a point of view is *right* sets something in motion and keeps it moving in the direction you have decided it should go. For instance, if you have the point of view that a successful business is a zero-sum game and that we live in a world of scarcity and lack rather than prosperity and abundance, then you will constantly create that as your reality. You won't see other possibilities because you have shut them out of your awareness with your point of view. Another way of saying this is that your point of view defines and creates your reality.

This *right way* is born from decisions, judgments, conclusions, assumptions, and preconceptions, which create limitation. Once you assume you have got something right, you don't think you need to change anything. Everywhere you look, what's reflected back at you is the rightness of you in any one moment, so you never seek change. We often believe that our point of view will prevail against all odds. We believe it will be proven to all that we are in the right, so we stick to our point of view until the bitter end. We all benefit by recognizing that we tend to automatically plunge into this entanglement. In effect, you contract your awareness and put on the filters of your bias and preconceived notions. For example, if you decide your business strategy or business model is the best in the world, can anything that isn't in that model come into your awareness? That would be *no.* You say, "This is all that is. This is all that exists." When you, as a business leader, see performance and success through the filter of the "right way to do things," you condemn your business and your staff to mediocrity because you are seeing things through the filters of your preconceptions. With every "rightness" and every "wrongness" you buy into, you are limiting your ability to receive abundantly and infinitely. Being mesmerized by the rightness of your point of view can actually kill your business.

The need to be right also plays out in our interpersonal rapport with our spouses and partners, where once again, it contracts our non-contextual awareness. Many people carry the need to be right into their personal interactions and create pointless arguments. Another manifestation of the need to be right is becoming vested in a particular outcome. You have a point of view about what the right outcome is. For example, when you conduct a business meeting, do you go in with the point of view that you must get a particular outcome? Or are you open to what is possible? When you are vested in an exact outcome or a specific result, you stop perceiving and receiving what else is possible. You only see the outcome you've decided on. You are unable to see anything that doesn't match it. As a result, what inevitably transpires is often less than what is truly possible. Can you imagine what it would be like if you were not vested in a specific outcome—and you were open to what is possible?

If you're looking to be right, triumphant, and successful, you may be looking for something that's worse than useless. It's actually damaging, because when you are invested in being right, you shut down your non-contextual awareness. Take a moment to consider the questions:

- *What's the value of holding on to this point of view?*

- *What point of view do you have that necessitates being right as your only possibility?*

- *Would you rather be right—or to have non-contextual awareness?*

What if the point of view you had didn't have to be a limitation?

What if the point of view you had was a possibility?

In Order to Be Right, You Have to Judge

As long as you have the point of view that you must to be right, you are going to be in judgment of your choices. That's because in order to be right, you have to judge. Then when you choose the "wrong" answer, you are wrong, and you feel compelled to make that right, ad infinitum. When you are in judgment of your choices, you blind yourself to all that actually is or could be. However, if you are willing to look at your choices without judgment, you will be able to see everything as it is. It's just what occurred. You can then say, "Okay, this is what occurring. May be right. May be wrong. How does it get any better than this?"

Alignment and Agreement, Resistance and Reaction

When we become mesmerized by the rightness of our point of view and function from judgment, what happens? We fall into the trap of alignment and agreement—or resistance and reaction. Alignment is: It's right, good, perfect, and correct. (This strategy is perfect. This business practice is correct. This point of view is correct—we don't need to consider anything else.) Resistance and reaction is: It's bad, wrong, mean, terrible, and awful. (This approach is wrong. This suggestion is awful. This idea is bad.)

If you have a judgment about anything, you automatically deny the better and more expansive options and possibilities that are available. You and others have to align and agree, or resist and react to the judgment. Therein lays much stress and misunderstanding. You are blinded to what is. Your employees will likely avoid being innovative or resourceful in order to avoid being criticized. A preoccupation with what is the "right way" and what is the "wrong way" is counterproductive to everything business leaders need to accomplish.

What if a choice was never right or wrong?

What if choices were just choices?

What if there is no right way and no wrong way—just ways, just different points of view?

What if every choice you make is not right or wrong but exactly what is required for you to become as aware as you truly are?

A judgment is not an inherent reality. It is always just a choice one makes. You can become the conscious and aware author of your own reality. You can look the world in the eye and declare, "I am choosing not to be a captive to my judgment of right, wrong, good, or bad anymore."

Allow Something Greater to Show Up

If you are willing to let go of the need to maintain the rightness of your point of view, you will eventually be released from the hypnotic power of contextual reality. As long as you spend your time trying to make your point of view right by aligning and agreeing with it, you have no reason to change because you think you've got everything right. In other words, your point of view allows you to maintain your self-comforting illusion of control. You make being right so important that you give up access to all the awareness you could have.

Everything we're taught in this reality is about judging, discerning, and looking at the rightness or the wrongness of things. What would your life would be like if you let go of your preferences and chose to have no point of view about anything?

Ultimate freedom lies in the awareness that a point of view is not right or wrong, good or bad. It's just an interesting point of view. Developing the ability to see every point of view as just an interesting point of view allows you to flow with the moment. You experience less stress and emotional turbulence. This ability doesn't develop overnight, but grows through dutiful practice and expanding awareness. Once you are willing to have totally no point of view about your life or what it is or isn't, you are actually free to generate any possibility you might choose.

Until you get to the awareness that everything is just an interesting point of view, you cannot truly observe; you can only judge. When you don't have the need to maintain the rightness of your point of view, there is nothing to fight. Seeing everything as just an interesting point of view is not simply a mindset. It's a form of behavior that guides everything you do. It can be a major strategic advantage.

The point is, two people engaged in the same meeting can have completely different perceptions and points of view of what the meeting means to them. It's essential to recognize this when you meet with others. Someone will believe one thing and you will believe something else. Does that make you right and them wrong? Does it make them right and you wrong? Or are they just different points of view? When you practice "interesting point of view" during a business meeting you will be able to observe what is going on with the people you are meeting with. You will see them in the light of how they truly are, without the filter of your thoughts, expectations, or judgments of how you think they should be.

If you can maintain "interesting point of view" in the face of disagreement and crisis, you have an enormous advantage over people. When you have no point of view and you present information to others, you create the space for them to change their point of view. However, if you have a point of view about what you are saying, people will tend to align and agree with you—or to fight you. Either way you are creating obstructions to seeing clearly.

Everything Is Just an Interesting Point Of View

Releasing ourselves from the hypnotic power of contextual reality is not a matter of exerting epic willpower. All that is required to release yourself from the hypnotic power of contextual reality (including false points of view, assumptions, judgments, and the need to be right) is a simple discipline of "everything is just an interesting point of view." The process itself is its own reward. When you allow yourself to be in "interesting point of view," your mind will become quiet and you will be able to perceive that other people are sitting in their own dilemmas. You will see that you don't have to react to them. You can be in total allowance of them, exactly as they are. If you don't do "interesting point of view," you align and agree with points of view—or you resist and react to them—which locks up your ability to perceive.

Our mentor, Gary Douglas, recommends to people that if they want to really get free, they should do one year of "interesting point of view that I have this point of view" for every point of view they have. By this he means, every time you find yourself expressing a point of view, you should say, "Interesting point of view that I have this point of view," which reminds you that nothing is fixed, true, or correct. You may think something is true or real—but it's only a point of view. It's not real.

When you function from "interesting point of view," you can't maintain fixed points of view. You immediately see that any point of view you have taken doesn't mean anything—and then you can change it. Every time you meet head-on with a strong viewpoint (whether it's yours or someone else's), you say to yourself, "Ah, interesting point of view." Whenever you catch yourself making judgments or having thoughts, inane drivel, or fixed points of view about anything, say to yourself, "Well, that's an interesting point of view." or "Interesting point of view I have this point of view."

Leaders who function from "everything is an interesting point of view" have seen profound improvement in their personal interactions, leadership ability, and family relations. Imagine what your business and your life would be like if you could function without judgment, without reasons, or justification and create a life that goes beyond the limitations of what the rest of the world thinks is important. When you don't judge what's right or wrong, every choice you make and every action you take can lead to new possibility.

Experience Total Choice and Total Possibility

Your world will expand exponentially as you let go of your viewpoints and become more aware of what is actually going on around you. The phrases "interesting point of view I think this" or "interesting point of view I am thinking this" can help you from getting stuck in fixed points of view.

If you do "interesting point of view I have this point of view" for every point of view you have, you will start moving into a place of no context. You will understand that the things you think are just points of view you have taken for the moment. You can change them. When you are able to step back from your own point of view, you have shifted from context into space. This is where you will experience total choice and total possibility. Try this for yourself. Once you are willing to let go of defending the rightness of your point of view about what something has to be, something greater can show up.

When you do not function from "interesting point of view," you tend to get caught up in the traumas and dramas of contextual reality. Is that where you want to live your life? The willingness to see everything as just an interesting point of view allows you to live your life from Question, Choice, Possibility, and Contribution. This is where the magic begins.

Lost in Identification with the Mind

Our society and cultural conditioning contextualize us. In contextual reality, people tend to function from thoughts, feelings, and emotions. What we think of as "truth" is an assemblage of points of view, conclusions, opinions, and judgments that we adopt as facts. It is essential to recognize that thoughts, feelings, and emotions are not facts, but a byproduct of the mind, which is the regulating system of our life. The mind is a calculating system that defines what we already are familiar with; it defines the limitations of our reality. The mind gets in the way of true knowing because it justifies everything we think and do. It induces us to define everything according to a linear construct that conforms to long-established human perspectives (contextual reality). It is designed to promote alignment and consistency, which can mutate into an unhealthy affection for conformity, where new possibilities are seen as a risky and a perilous option.

Most of us tend to identify with our thoughts, feelings, and emotions as though they are who we are. This is a misperception. You are not your thoughts, feelings, or emotions. Treating thoughts, feelings, and emotions as real, significant, or true can be a big problem for business leaders.

Verify this notion for yourself. Observe yourself throughout the day to see how you operate when you identify with your thoughts, feelings, and emotions—and how you operate when you recognize them as simply an interesting point of view. Try the following exercise. When you find yourself lost in identification with your mind, thoughts, feelings, and emotions, ask yourself:

What am I making real and significant here?

Are you more effective when you notice that thoughts, feelings, and emotions come and go, while who you truly are remains? Or are you more effective when you identify with your mind, thoughts, feelings, and emotions and believe they are true?

Reflection

Observe yourself throughout the day to see if you are leading your life and your business from the perspective of contextual reality. Are you always looking for where you fit, how you benefit, where you can win, and how to avoid losing?

You cannot master your life from contextual reality. You can only master it from a non-contextual awareness. You can't maneuver your influence dynamically or masterfully if you have allowed yourself to be under the control of the hypnotic power of contextual reality.

The Mind Gets in the Way of Knowing

Knowing is the intelligent flow of insight that transpires instantaneously once the mind and emotions are balanced, calm, and coherent. Once you wipe out your mind as the regulating system of your life, you can function from knowing. We've all had those moments, when with the snap of our fingers, we knew everything. Can we think ourselves into those positions? No—that's not where the mind takes us. It actually moves us in the opposite direction.

Knowing is awareness of what the possibilities are without having any judgment about them. With knowing, you are aware of what you or others are—or are not—willing to choose or receive. You are aware of what will result from your choices. When you choose to follow your knowing, you will move toward that which expands your life.

Would you be willing to see that your contextual mind justifies everything you do and does nothing to create infinite possibilities? Everywhere you have made thinking greater than knowing would you destroy and uncreate that, please?

Knowing Is Not a Product of Thought

When you are thinking or you are "in your head," you are not functioning from your knowing. Functioning from knowing means you stop identifying with your thinking mind, which is only a small aspect of the consciousness that you are. When the mind is immersed in compulsive thinking, you cannot get in touch with your deeper knowing. Any fixed point of view, prejudice, or judgment of any kind indicates you are identifying with the thinking mind. The deep knowing that is insight arises through the simple act of giving your full attention to whatever you are doing and being in the moment. When you're totally aware, you receive all the information.

Knowing is different from knowledge. Knowledge is the idea that you have to learn something in order to know it. This is not correct. To know, you simply have to ask questions. You ask a question to get the knowing, not the answer. Questions expand your knowing. Trying to get to the answer diminishes your knowing and stops everything dead in its tracks.

Would you rather have the false sense of security that comes from having the right answer—or would you rather have the knowing that allows you to access infinite possibilities?

When you ask yourself this question, you may discover that you have an attachment to getting the right answer. You are hanging on to the false sense of security that comes from having an answer or thinking you know what to expect. You can choose that—or you can choose to be open to the uncertainty that comes from letting go of your points of view about what something has to be.

If you answered that you would rather have the knowing, we invite you to let go of your attachment to having the right answer. If you have a hard time embracing this notion, would you be willing to remain open at least to the *possibility* that letting go of your attachment to having the right answer might be of service to you?

Trust Your Knowing

Being aware and present in the moment dissolves the barriers created by your mind. If you would like to generate no-more-business-as-usual, you have to embrace your knowing and stop identifying with your thinking mind. In practice, this means redesigning your business strategies around the unconventional principles of non-contextual awareness.

Every time you choose from a conscious place by following your knowing, you generate a plethora of possibilities. Every time you go against your knowing, you kill every possibility that you could generate for your business. You cannot go against what you know without destroying your business. We encourage you to approach your life by following your knowing. In fact, if you make it a practice to follow your knowing as you go about your daily life, even with the small stuff, you will move towards that which expands your life and possibilities. If you ask the question "Am I pretending not to know, denying that I know, or actually knowing?", you'll bypass your cognitive mind and step away from your thoughts, feelings and emotions. Be persistent. The more you follow your knowing, the more naturally it will become an alternative to thinking.

Have you ever had the experience of knowing you shouldn't take up that project, create that product, hire that person, or go into that business deal? You knew it was going to turn out badly, and you did it anyway. How did it turn out? Just as bad as you knew it was going to turn out? In order to go against your knowing, you have to cut off your awareness of everything else. In this instance, instead of following what you knew, you turned to contextual reality for direction. You must be willing to receive the information in front of you. You have to be willing to let go of any standards or expectations (fixed points of view) and allow yourself to receive everything from everyone without judgment. If you are going into a meeting, before you walk in, you can ask:

Who is here in front of me?

What's going on?

What are they doing?

When you are willing to receive all the information, you will know what's going on. You can also ask:

Does this feel light or heavy?

This is your cue to what's true for you and what's a lie. If you consistently use the tool, "if it's light it is right, and if it's heavy it is a lie," you will know what is true for you, what works for you, and what is right for you in that moment. When somebody tells you something and it makes you feel lighter, you'll know it's true for you. If it feels heavy, you can ask "What's the lie?" or "What lie am I buying here?"

Your job as a leader is to make sure that your leadership team is functioning with conscious awareness and to exemplify continuous renewal and transformation. To do this, you have to expand your ability to perceive all that is happening around you without buying thoughts, biases, and feelings as real. Trust your knowing.

Unconscious Conditioning

Our cultural conditioning and entrained points of view maintain our contextual reality. Where we grew up, how we grew up, and everything we experienced as we grew up become the programming that sets us up for not being. We can't see this because we have been brainwashed. Our unconscious conditioning creates limitations in our life by limiting what we can perceive, know, be, and receive. We don't realize we can do this from choice and "beingness".

This unconscious conditioning poses particular problems in setting business strategy because it sets us up to automatically go into conclusion, judgment, discrimination, and discernment. It causes us to assume that trends will continue pretty much as they always have. We tend to take the status quo for granted rather than question our assumptions. As a result, we underestimate the long-term effect of new technologies, environmental crises, and globalization. Sadly, too much of what gets done in most companies is in response unconscious conditioning and holding on to past reference points. That's why so many companies end up trapped in the conventional business-as-usual paradigm.

Most people have problems processing new ideas because of unconscious conditioning. That's why certain things are always perceived the same way. Our unconscious conditioning is an automatic habitual brain function that we substitute for awareness. It is as if we are addicted to contextual reality. To generate our business on the edge of possibility we have to break the old habits of this unconscious conditioning.

Reflection

Ask yourself these questions:

> *In what ways do my business practices and strategies conform and reinforce a constricted view of contextual reality?*
>
> *How do they create limitation for my business?*
>
> *What systems surround and govern my organization?*
>
> *Is my organization bound by a consensual set of constraints that limits my ability to address new opportunities?*

Engage in asking these questions from a place of curiosity. Treat it as an exploration of everything that is truly possible for you. If you will destroy and un-create all your conditioning and programmed points of view, a new possibility can show up in your life. From this space you are now free to turn to the questions:

What's possible here?

What choice do I have?

What question is there that will expand my life?

What contribution can I be?

As you reflect on these questions, you may experience yourself gradually gaining a new perspective of what else is possible—and you will also become aware of the exquisiteness of what is already here now in the present moment. This is the point from which new possibilities begin to emerge.

CHAPTER EIGHT

Unshackle Yourself From Contextual Reality

Few people are capable of expressing with equanimity opinions which differ from the prejudices of their social environment. Most people are even incapable of forming such opinions.
~ *Albert Einstein*

Organizations that operate based on the conventional business-as-usual paradigm are prisoners of contextual reality. They are captives to their efficiency-centric, bureaucracy-based contextual paradigms. They're bound by precedent—and the majority of them have a vested interest in the business-as-usual status quo. Put simply, contextual reality dictates the way conventional business leaders do business, and it does so in a way that makes organization performance predictable and unsurprising.

The Peril of Contextual Mindsets

There is a state of mind we'd like to acquaint you with. We call it the contextual mindset. Perhaps you are already familiar with this insidious disposition. You are being seduced by contextual mindsets if:

You think in terms of what is not possible

You act in ways that are acceptable and predictable

You think things are pretty good the way they are, no matter how dismal and grim the circumstance is.

Contextual mindsets induce you to relinquish what is truly possible in exchange for efficiency and expediency. They coerce you to conduct your business within certain boundaries and limitations. They prompt you to do what is projected and anticipated and what has worked in the past. Contextual mindsets are never innovative. They can't be—because having contextual mindsets means conforming and operating along the lines of your current business.

Leaders who are seduced by contextual mindsets need predictability. They hate change. They abhor uncertainty, chaos, and unpredictability, and they tend to do everything they can to keep their business from evolving. Many of them even invent obstructions designed to slow the evolution of their business so they can gradually adjust to what's going on. This is about control, not about awareness. When leaders have trepidation about change, they're likely to avoid taking risks. They try to figure out how to control their businesses so they can fit, benefit, win, and avoid losing.

The movie *The Matrix* gives us hints about how contextual reality works. A contextual mindset tells us the status quo is what we want. It influences us not to make waves, it impels us to keep things the same, it drives us to refuse to change things, and convinces us everything is going to be the same forever. It keeps us in the illusion that the businesses we are creating are just fine, even though somewhere in our universe it may not feel fine.

Contextual mindsets drive our thoughts and beliefs and most importantly our choices, which most often are not choices at all, but hidden forces that shape our realities.

Conscious leaders know that if they do not resist and react to the change that is on its way that they will be aware of where to be and what to do about the change that is coming. They face change straight on. They look at it for themselves and realize, "If I'm not willing to embrace evolutionary change, then what I'm saying is I don't want to be any different." Are you aware of that? If you are not willing to have evolutionary change occur, you don't actually allow the change your business is demanding.

To escape the trap of the contextual mindset, you have to be able to rise above it. You have to look at what *is* and not assume something is true based on your judgments of what is right and perfect. "Right and perfect" is the distinguishing view of the contextual mindset. It's a judgment that causes us to refuse to perceive, know, be, or receive the infinite possibilities that are available.

Why You Are Blindsided

All of your learning up until now has probably been about how to be in context with this reality. Our society is designed to keep us in contextual reality and always choosing based on where we fit, how we benefit, where we win, and how to not lose. Our entire upbringing has been about how to be in context with this reality.

Many business executives doubt that it's possible to be successful outside the confines of contextual reality. They believe that the immutable laws of contextual reality constrain the range of choices and options for engendering financial success. They assume that an industry's structural conditions are constrained by contextual reality and that they are forced to compete within them. They thus put themselves into a no-choice position. They tend to spend much of their time sitting in judgment, trying to figure out how to function in the labyrinth so they can get along in the world.

You may ask, "What's wrong with functioning within contextual reality if things are going well for me?" Maybe you are mostly satisfied with your life and your level of business. You know how to handle it and you know where you fit in the scheme of things. You may be thinking, "I don't know if I want to change the way things are. I like it this way. I feel safe and secure. I have accepted the rules of contextual reality and made peace with the status quo. I prefer it when things remain constant and stable." We can see your point. When your business is humming along and things are going well, you probably don't see the need to change or question accepted business paradigms. When things are going well, most leaders don't want to rock the boat. They certainly don't want to take actions that defy their apparent ultimate framework that is grounded in certainty.

In our view, this mindset is fraught with danger—if not right now, then soon. Here's why. When you are seduced by contextual reality, you tend to be myopic. You concentrate on the business close at hand. You don't see the many signs that could mean change is coming in your business model or industry.

Potentially great organizations are crippled by leaders who refuse to be aware of the new hyper-change world and continue to manage their business-as-usual. Here is a profile of leaders who are seduced by conceptual reality:

- *They abandon their awareness and operate on autopilot.*

- *They filter out unwanted signals and other possibilities.*

- *They reject the signs that business is being shifted or needs to be shifted.*

- *They refuse to see change as critical to their business.*

- *They ignore the evidence that something needs to change.*

- *They consider changes in technology to be disruptive but temporary.*

- *They believe their organization will be in a satisfactory position once disruptive changes blow over.*

- *They are proud of their past successes (and are possibly trapped in them).*

- *They continue to look backward for reference points they can understand.*

- *They make judgment calls, trade-offs, and compromises that harm their organization.*

Do you see any of these qualities in yourself? Can you imagine what it would be like if you could liberate yourself from the contextual mindset and function from non-contextual awareness? What if you were adept at perceiving, knowing, being, and receiving? What if you lived in the question and not the answer? What if you operated from allowance and interesting point of view rather than judgment? What if you were a true leader and not a follower? What else might be possible?

Four Disciplines

Four disciplines guaranteed to unshackle you from contextual mindsets are:

1. *Be present to contextual reality*

2. *Be willing to receive everything without judgment*

3. *Be flexible and adaptable*

4. *Renounce the right vs. wrong paradigm*

Choosing to unshackle yourself from contextual mindsets is an internal process. That is, it has nothing to do with anything or anyone else except you. It is making the commitment not to live by anyone else's judgment (including your own) ever again, no matter what.

1. Be Present to Contextual Reality

The gravitational pull of contextual reality is strong indeed. It is the environment in which most people reside. To bring possibility forth into contextual reality, we have to develop an ability to be present to it. You will be a victim of the people who function in contextual reality if you are not able to be present to it. You have to look at what is. This is about being aware and sensitive to context. Awareness and acknowledgement of context and its influence are vitally important parts of what you can bring to a situation. Being shackled by contextual reality is a self-imposed choice. You have the power to release yourself from it and use it to your advantage, from awareness.

In other words, contextual reality is not something you have to eliminate. This world functions from the "fit, benefit, win, lose" parameters of contextual reality. You can't live outside of contextual reality and still function in society. You can't get rid of it or destroy it. You have to be able to live with it—but you don't have to buy it as real and true. It is about being functional within this reality. How do you do this?

First, recognize the existence of contextual reality. Next, acknowledge that contextual reality just *is*. Releasing yourself from the control of the contextual mindset is not about judging that contextual reality is wrong or that there's something bad or evil about it. It's about being present to contextual reality without resistance. This is not the same as accepting contextual reality as real and true. Being without resistance does not mean you allow the contextual mindset to control you. If you ever studied martial arts, you may remember whenever you let go of resistance you have greater power and potency and greater awareness, openness, and alertness.

Resistance is actually quite insidious. In order to be in resistance to contextual reality, you need to have previously agreed and aligned with it to some extent, and then at a later point, gone into resistance of it. Either of those extremes—agreement and alignment (it's right, good, perfect, and correct) or resistance and reaction (it's bad, wrong, mean, terrible, and awful)—locks you up. Either way you are judging. And as long as you are judging, you are giving up the awareness of what your choice will create.

Are you wondering about how to put this into practice in your life? If you wish to truly be present to contextual reality (or anything else) you have to be willing to receive everything without judgment. We mean everything. You have to be willing to receive any energy, whatever the energy is. You also have to be willing to perceive, know, and be everything. Anything else diminishes your ability to be present. It is only what you have decided you cannot receive that limits what you can have in life.

2. Be Willing to Receive Everything

Receiving is the ability to be in allowance of everything and everyone exactly as they are. You do not resist or react to any interaction with anything or anyone. You don't agree and align with anything or anyone. You are constantly open, vulnerable, and unresisting to any energy. You are able to receive everything and everyone with true gratitude and without any sense of obligation, judgment, or filtering. Infinite possibility is about receiving. Any avoidance of any receiving is an avoidance of consciousness.

Whenever your life is not working as well as you would like, there is always an unwillingness to receive something. At the bottom of any problem is an unwillingness to receive. When you are unwilling to receive, you withdraw from being in communion with others and from all things. Would you be willing to see what is not working in your life and in your business? Ask yourself:

Is there anything that I am not willing to receive?

What am I absolutely unwilling to receive?

You have to be willing to receive all information to know what the choices and possibilities are. How can you make choices for yourself and your business without this information? For instance, when you go into a business meeting, do you go in with a preconceived or predetermined idea that you must achieve a particular result? (Do you see how this shuts out your awareness of what's possible?) Or are you open and willing to receive whatever comes your way? If you don't have any expectation of a specific result you have to achieve, you will be able to receive what is possible.

What then tends to show up is even more than you imagined or expected. Receiving is receiving information, money, possibilities, and everything else under the sun.

Be willing to receive everything can come into your life, including the judgment of others. Willingness to receive everything without judgment is a form of sustenance and awareness that empowers you. It is the most generative power that you can seize, in that it opens up new avenues, pathways, and possibilities that have previously eluded you. A key part of being willing to receive everything is to stop resisting and reacting to any interaction you or anyone else has. Choose to let go of all resistance to any energy, thoughts, feelings, and emotions. Have no resistance, no rejection, no negation, and no refusal of any concept or relationship. This means no projection, expectation, judgment, rejection, and separation in your mind— and the willingness to be fully aware of everything. Projection, expectation, judgment, rejection, and separation generate irrational fears that can induce a toxic and destructive state within you. The remedy for this is to be willing to receive everything. When you catch yourself resisting and reacting, ask the following questions:

> *What am I unwilling to receive here?*
>
> *What ideas or viewpoints have I created that are stopping me from receiving? (Note that these ideas and viewpoints may seem very meaningful—but that doesn't mean they are true.)*

When you are willing to be present to the falsehood of contextual reality and to perceive and receive it without judgment, you will no longer be the effect of it. If you are not willing to be present to contextual reality without judgment, you will not perceive what people are going to do in this contextual reality. If you are not willing to receive and be in allowance of all that, then you either think that the energy you perceive is you and something you are choosing, or you go into it to find out why someone would choose it. That's what confuses and sidetracks you. The willingness to receive all the energies of contextual reality will allow them to come to you, and they don't affect you.

3. Be Flexible and Adaptable

Over the coming decades, the flexibility of every leader and organization will be tested as never before. The ability of organizations to prosper and thrive depends on their capacity to operate from the edge of possibility. While many leaders readily acknowledge that it is essential to be flexible, they often assume that business vision, mission, and values need to be undeviating, stable, and enduring. Organizations miss new possibilities when leaders operate from these fixed positions. These leaders are unaware that harnessing the ability to change leads to amazing growth and unlimited opportunities.

It is dangerous for leaders to be fixed in their points of view because they tend to cling to familiar territory and stereotypical behavior. They turn a blind eye toward a changing environment. They often see the business of today and the future as being very much like the business of the past. The truth is that change is taking place whether we like it or not. It is prevailing, proliferating, and accelerating.

Leaders with fixed points of view often feel defensive and limited, and they often create an unhealthy culture in their organization that is characterized by polarized views about what is right, wrong, good, or bad. The more rigid they are, the more risk-averse they become. One of the best predictors of an organization's health is how well the chief executive and leadership team adapt and respond to changes. In today's swiftly evolving and increasingly changeable world, organizations cannot afford to deploy leaders with fixed points of view.

Indeed most businesses fail because of the fixed points of view that their leaders take. The degree to which leaders function from fixed points of view is in direct proportion to their inability to innovate. A fixed point of view often generates professional complacency, squashes initiatives, promotes unthinking compliance, and cultivates an unconscious organization. These leaders are prime candidates for executive derailment. They harm themselves, their organization, and others around them.

If you have a fixed point of view about anything, you automatically deny the possibilities that there are better and more expansive things available. Great opportunities in business always come from occurrences and events that are happening now. If you are blinded by your fixed points of view, you won't see the opportunities until it's too late. In fact, you won't see anything that doesn't match your point of view. Once you have a fixed point of view, you then have created a box to self-limit what is possible, and you and others have to align and agree, or resist and react. Therein lies much stress and misunderstanding.

Fixed points of view will lead you nowhere but into mediocrity. They will crush the life out of your business as swiftly as changing market environments. If you're having difficulties achieving your target, you may be sticking with a strategy that is based on a fixed point of view that is no longer workable. If you acknowledge this, you can have other choices. Everything is available to you when you acknowledge without judgment what you are doing and being.

If you are repeating the same thoughts over and over in response to circumstances, people, and conditions, this is a sure sign of a fixed point of view in action. Fixed points of view are nothing more than beliefs and ideas you think of as real, permanent, and true. All you have to do is to become aware of the fixed position that you have been imposing on yourself, your business, and others. Once you've identified what your fixed points of view are, you need to catch yourself in the act of having them—and recognize them for what they are, without judgment. You can then choose to step outside your fixed points of view and thought patterns. One simple way to do this is ask yourself a question that short-circuits your mind:

> *What if everything is opposite of what it appears to be and nothing is the opposite of what it appears to be?*

Keep asking yourself this question and you will get out of that fixed-point-of-view space.

4. Renounce the Right vs. Wrong Paradigm

A fixed point of view often spawns the right vs. wrong paradigm, which creates separation and divides an organization. A fixed point of view frequently gives rise to a fixation on proving that you are right by asserting that others are wrong. Each time you identify with your point of view, you have to make it right and you automatically and unconsciously try to defend it against others. The majority of your energy is spent defending this point of view. Oftentimes the compulsion to be "right" suppresses innovation, originality, and creativity in the name of organizational effectiveness.

Perhaps the biggest block to being successful is your point of view of right, wrong, good, or bad. When your mind is relentlessly going on about how wrong or how right things are, you diminish your ability to take action. And whenever you judge something, information that doesn't already match your judgment cannot come into your awareness. When you have a fixed point of view that something is correct and right, or something is terrible and wrong, there is no room for something else to show up.

New and different possibilities in business always come from changes that are taking place right here and right now. If the right vs. wrong paradigm blinds you, you won't perceive the changes until it's too late. This is what happens to many business leaders. Because of their points of view of right, wrong, good, or bad, they are unable to perceive, know, be, or receive the infinite possibilities that are available.

What if there was no such thing as right or wrong, good or bad?

There is a parable that captures the notion of the question, "What if there was no such thing as right or wrong, good or bad?"

There was once a young man who came from a very poor family in China. Once when he was out for the day, his horse ran away. On his return, the villagers went to his father to express their sadness for this financial loss.

"Such a great loss. Isn't this terrible?" they wailed. The aged father shook his head from side to side and calmly stated, "You never know. May be good. May be bad."

On the following day, the lad went out to hunt for the missing steed. To his great joy, he found a herd of wild horses and was able to bring them back to the village. The elated crowd ran to his father and exclaimed, "Isn't this wonderful news? What great fortune!" The sage-like elder again merely stated, "You never know. May be good. May be bad."

The next morning the boy went out into the corral to try to break in a horse for himself. In the process he was trampled and made lame. When the townspeople saw his ruined leg, they ran to his father to convey their grief. The reply was the same again, "You never know. May be good. May be bad."

Soon after this, war broke out in the land and all the young men were conscripted into the army, except the farmer's son, who couldn't go because of his damaged leg. A day or so later the Chinese army came to take all the able-bodied young men away to war. After the army left without taking the son, the elated crowd ran to his father and exclaimed, "Isn't this wonderful news? What a great piece of luck." The sage-like elder again merely stated, "You never know. May be good. May be bad."

What if you adopted the mindset that there was no such thing as right or wrong, good or bad? Can you imagine what your life would be like if you could live with the point of view, "You never know. May be good. May be bad." If you become like the father in the parable and you have no judgment of anything, you get to look at everything for what it is—not for what you want it to be, not for what you think it ought to be.

We have adopted this practice in our own life. When unforeseen things occur in our daily life or in our business, we often look at each other, smile and say, "You never know. May be good. May be bad. How does it get any better than this?" And when things seem to be really ominous and threatening we ask, "What are the infinite possibilities that this could work out better than we could ever imagine?"

Would you be willing to see that right and wrong, good and bad are judgments and conclusions? It is the things that we consider right, good, perfect, and/or correct that stick us the most, because we do not wish to let go of them or we have no apparent reason for doing so. Most people find it much easier to look for the things that feel wrong, bad, imperfect, or incorrect to ease their pain and suffering. These perspectives generally evolve from some strong unconscious programming that has come about in response to similar situations in a completely different context. By and large, the situation had some forceful emotional context and disturbing corollaries associated with it. Possibly you had a massive win or a gargantuan loss, which caused the point of view to get locked into your universe. However, all that is irrelevant, because that was then; it's not now. Unless you can look at what was and see how you agreed or disagreed with it or how you were horrified by it or helped by it—and then release yourself from that point of view—you will be stuck by it forever. It is simply a choice.

Another way you can release yourself from the right vs. wrong paradigm is to use the question:

What am I not getting about this?

Our initial tendency is to ask, "What's wrong with this?" When we ask, "What am I not getting about this?" we start to perceive things in a new way. It's not that we are looking for an intellectual answer. "What am I not getting about this?" encourages us look at the opportunities in our situation rather than focusing on what's wrong. What if every situation is an opportunity for more awareness?

Whenever you catch yourself having a positive or negative mindset about anything (or when you find yourself aligning and agreeing with a point of view—or resisting and reacting to it), ask:

What if there was no such thing as right or wrong, good or bad?

What am I making solid, real and true here?

Looking at Things from a Different Point of View

Unshackling yourself from contextual mindsets is about looking at things from a slightly different point of view, where nothing affects you negatively and you don't buy into the agreements of contextual reality.

Most of us don't realize how much our point of view determines our choices, and many of us don't realize how fixed and unconstructive contextual mindsets can be. So with every fixed point of view you have, every "rightness" that you believe, every "wrongness" that you believe, you are limiting your ability to receive abundantly and infinitely.

Reflection

Some fundamental questions for you to consider are:

How much of your life have you lived based on fixed points of view, the right vs. wrong paradigm and past reference points?

Do you define your business so it fits the context of this reality?

Do you always look for the negative reference points in life?

Do you always look for what you have not or are not, to determine what you should or should not do?

It can be challenging to discharge ingrained fixed points of view when you can't see them for what they are. Be brutally honest with yourself and choose to become aware of the points of view you hold that are based in contextual reality. If you want freedom in this area, you have to be intensely truthful with yourself. Are you willing to look at what is trapping you, no matter what it is? Notice when you read this question, that there will be an answer. What came up for you? Was it *yes* or *no*? If you don't want to look at what's trapping you, that's okay. You can acknowledge that and move on. Unless you are willing to make the demand, "no matter what it takes I'm examining this and changing it," nothing can change. Consciousness can only be experienced when you choose to become aware of your own way of being.

Once you are able to unshackle yourself from the hypnotic power of contextual reality, you will begin to function from a place of possibility and awareness, and you can cultivate the ability to be functional with contextual reality. As you'll see in subsequent chapters, when you are being functional with contextual reality, things come together quickly and easily and fall into place instantaneously. Being functional with contextual reality is the way to the freedom and choice. It creates space for you to generate anything you would like in your business and your life.

CHAPTER NINE

Being Functional With Contextual Reality

Here's to the crazy ones, the misfits, the rebels, the troublemakers, the round pegs in the square holes... the ones who see things differently... they're not fond of rules... You can quote them, disagree with them, glorify or vilify them, but the only thing you can't do is ignore them because they change things... they push the human race forward, and while some may see them as the crazy ones, we see genius, because the ones who are crazy enough to think that they can change the world, are the ones who do.
~Think Different, narrated by Steve Jobs

In the current economic environment, the key skill that ensures your staying power in business is the ability to be functional with this contextual reality. This ability defines the difference between those who limit themselves to a business-as-usual existence and those who triumph over limitations in remarkable ways and achieve phenomenal results. Indeed, being functional with this contextual reality may be a requirement for creating exceptional accomplishments. Steve Jobs, Warren Buffet, Jeff Immelt, and Richard Branson are four well-known examples of individuals who have this ability. Social entrepreneur Bill Strickland is another. In the midst of a complex and fast-changing field of business, these leaders have expanded their awareness to perceive and receive what is going on around them. They have an intrinsic capacity to perceive, know, and receive the stimuli that shape the times in which they live—and to seize on the resulting opportunities.

So, What Exactly Is Being Functional with this Contextual Reality?

Being functional with this contextual reality is the ability to rise above what's going on and to clearly see behavior, attitudes, approaches, and events as contextual. In other words, being aware of this contextual reality when it unfolds around you (one will perceive contextual reality in many different spheres: in oneself, in one's organization, among clients or customers, in industry, in the world at large). Simply put, it is the same as seeing others going about business-as-usual. When you are being functional with contextual reality, you are above it and you see there are things that require your attention. When you are functional, you are willing to change what you are able to change and don't try to deal with what you can't change.

Most traditional business training, practices, and techniques have been about how to be in context with this reality. If your board and your leadership team are always looking for where they fit, how they benefit, where they can win, and how to avoid losing, your business is certainly operating within this contextual reality. Contextual reality creates a world of judgments and beliefs. Operating from this contextual reality as though it is real is the only way to create business as limited. Businesses that obsessively seek to be in context with this reality are often self-defeating and self-destructive. The real problem with being in context with this reality is that it dilutes innovation and the impetus to make remarkable things in the first place. It lets organizations hide from the profound challenges of making insanely great contributions that are truly possible. Being in context with this reality offers a kind of insurance to businesses: Many companies believe that if they can find diverse ways to sell products or services, they don't have to make better products or develop new services. For example, the 1990s and 2000s have been full of companies churning out the same old toxic, noxious products and trying to sell them in new ways—instead of purifying them. When businesses invest in looking for where they fit, how they benefit, where they can win, and how to avoid losing, they often try to sell things better, instead of producing better products or services.

The key to becoming functional with this contextual reality is non-contextual awareness (refer to Chapter 6). The good news is that it is possible for everyone to increase their zone of non-contextual awareness if they choose. To step into being functional with contextual reality and into success requires you to go into question and non-contextual awareness. With non-contextual awareness, you have choice. This is an important concept to get because it's what prevents you from having the success you desire in many areas of your life. In order to live in this contextual reality and to live under that pretence of what this reality is, people tend to cut off their zone of non-contextual awareness. People who shrink their zone of non-contextual awareness will not be able to see beyond current contextual realities. They will not be able to perceive the opportunities and will not sense the weak spots or dilemmas that their organization may encounter. To be functional with this contextual reality you have to ask questions. Everything must be a question for you, a whole life of questions. You cannot do a decision, conclusion, or judgment about anything. The moment you come to conclusion you get connected back into contextual reality, you have limited what you can receive. You can ask, "What's possible here? What would I like to choose?" If you have to deal with people who operate within this contextual reality, you can also ask, "How do I use where these people function from to my advantage?" When you're being the question with everything, you can have total awareness of it. For example, when you are in business meeting, what you need to do is be in non-contextual awareness with the people you are meeting with. From non-contextual awareness, you have choice. You can ask, "What's possible here? What is possible with this meeting? What would I like to choose? I can let them be close to me or reject them or I can use that to get whatever I want. What contribution can they be to my business and what contribution can I be to them? What choices do we have? What question will open the door to more?"

You cannot operate from an automatic system or an autopilot mode if you are choosing to be functional with this contextual reality, there is always a moment where you can make a different choice. If you ask every day: "What do I need to be aware of today? Is there someplace I need to put my energy or my attention today?" From that space, allow yourself to receive the awareness of different possibilities and then put whatever energy or attention you need to put there in order to keep things moving. That's operating from non-contextual awareness. That's operating beyond contextual reality. That's being functional with this contextual reality, outside of the contextual reality, because you're actually in the question.

A Simple and Powerful Premise

In a world where the pace of change is accelerating frantically, being functional with this contextual reality is crucial. Business genius is much more than aptitude, experience, skill, talent, and ability. Talent and ability may merely be one faculty developed out of proportion to other faculties, but real genius is the ability to operate beyond contextual reality as well as being functional with contextual reality.

Being functional with this contextual reality is completely different from operating within the standards and the confinement of contextual reality. Organizations that have leaders who are functional with contextual reality consistently outperform others by taking advantage of new possibilities. They know how to act quickly and how to employ contextual reality to their advantage. This is because they are able to rise above what's going on, beyond their past success, beyond the walls of the organization, and even beyond their industry sector and market precinct to capture the intangibles. They have the ability to perceive the intangibles that differentiate and transform. They are also able to see the way other people are ensnared by contextual reality, and they use this awareness to their advantage.

The key to this is to perceive things differently by expanding your awareness. You can keep asking: What do I need to be aware of here? What's possible here? What would I like to choose? It may concern emerging trends in markets that a company serves, or it may be innovative development in a part of the world the company barely pays attention to, or other emerging shifts in the environment globally. Obviously, it is vital to pay serious attention to the emerging trends and shifts in the market. It can be a source of new possibilities, the area of strategic advantage, or a source of tactical faux pas.

General Electric's CEO Jeff Immelt demonstrates what it means to employ contextual reality to the advantage of General Electric (GE). Jeff Immelt uses the awareness that many people in the Western world are becoming more concerned about the environment, particularly global warming. From this awareness, GE set a new growth strategy to seize the new opportunities to benefit from energy concerns. The company came up with the "Ecomagination," a new strategy that reflects the company's commitment to "invest in a future that creates innovative solutions to environment challenges and delivers valuable products and services to customers while generating profitable growth for the company" (GE Ecomagination Report 2008).

GE seized the opportunity and initiated products and services to increase social, human, and environmental impacts which allow them to realize higher financial performance. The innovative solutions include things like solar generators, nuclear power plants, and wind turbines. With this strategy, General Electric released itself from the control of contextual reality while being functional within it. For GE, the Ecomagination strategy yields business value and financial success from quantifiable improvements like energy and water efficiency as well as better quality of life.

Another standout example is FedEx, who has lucratively and effectively benefited from the new options created by the Internet and the shifting demands of their customers. By looking at the edges of traditional mail delivery, FedEx created an industry in overnight delivery. They found new opportunities in handling global components that emerged from the convergence of trends in global freight flow, outsourcing demands, and Internet availability. They are doing what is unexpected, unforeseen, and unpredictable, and going beyond what is normal. They defy the norms of conventional practice.

To consistently function from this space you must be open to receive and perceive emerging trends outside your organization's primary area of focus. Simply put, you must open yourself up to hearing about, observing, and discovering new possibilities and opportunities. You have to be willing to dynamically explore new ways to think about the market, emerging technologies, and new ways of operating the business. In order to thrive in the global knowledge economy, where innovation and originality will be rewarded, business leaders have to think differently about how they approach business choices. You can expand your awareness with a stimulating question: What emerging new trends could replace our current business? With this question, you will expand your scope beyond traditional business, beyond current customers and competitors, and consider the broader social and regulatory forces that could reshape the environment.

Being functional with this contextual reality allows organizations like General Electric, FedEx, and Apple Inc. to simultaneously perceive where they want to be as well as where they are. It allows them to see life as an extraordinary adventure, to experience life in a serendipitous state, and to create themselves new in every moment. It is about being indefinable, and not creating their businesses based on identity, definition, or past reference points. What this means is to no longer live by the rules of this reality, but to live at the generative edge of possibility, to be open to life in such a way that celebration becomes your natural state of being.

What Does This Mean in Practice?

Employ your awareness. Being functional with contextual reality means employing your awareness to make contextual reality work for you. You have to see when you or others are captivated by contextual reality. Being captivated means doing what others have done before. It's following the norms, aligning your business with conventional business models, and basing your decisions on benchmarking and historical trends or earlier success. You are unlikely to become functional within contextual reality if you're standing in the mainstream and are unaware that you are being captivated by contextual reality.

To create space to do this, you first have to be aware of the business orthodoxies and management dogmas that are based on contextual reality. You have to cultivate the ability to sit above what's going on and be willing to perceive all the things that require your attention. To be functional with this contextual reality, you must be willing to change what you are able to change and most importantly don't try to deal with what you can't change. *Use these four questions for everything: What is this? What do I do with it? Can I change it? How can I change it?* Look for the assumptions in routines, processes, and procedures that determine how management and operations get carried out on a day-to-day basis. Typical processes include strategic planning, financial planning and budgeting, project management, internal communications, human resource processes, performance reviews and assessments. These processes tend to shape an organization's culture by reinforcing certain behaviors and not others. It's not easy to change an organization's culture without changing the processes that govern work. Look at how your processes may blind you and your organization to new possibilities.

Especially important is your willingness to be aware of information, particularly that which is new and even disconcerting. Information must actively be sought from everywhere, from places and sources you never thought to look before. You don't just look for information that makes you feel good, that verifies past success and validates your present endeavors. You consciously and intentionally look for information that might threaten your stability, knock your organization off balance, and open it to growth and new possibilities.

Don't judge contextual reality. It's not about judging contextual reality as wrong. (Remember: Consciousness includes everything and judges nothing.) If you have the judgment that contextual reality is wrong, can you effectively function with it and use it to your advantage? No. If you have no judgment of it, can you make contextual reality work for you? Yes. You can observe what is going on in the business environment around you and ask: How do I use where these people function from to my advantage?"

Ask non-contextual questions. Remaining open-minded is a start, but you have to go further by asking questions designed to understand a rapidly changing field when you're not even sure what part is changing. The power to truly be functional with contextual reality hinges on the ability to ask non-contextual questions. These questions are different from conventional questions that relate to business functions such as, What is our market share? What is our profit? Non-contextual questions indicate curiosity and a sense exploration. It's looking at what else is possible and seeking to examine current

Asking non-contextual questions requires an open mind, a willingness to receive uncertainty, and the audacity to explore and investigate unfamiliar territory. Non-contextual questions allow you to perceive, know, be, and receive new ways to think about the market, emerging technologies, and new business practices. They can help you identify unseen opportunities as well as risks. Questions allow you to see beyond traditional business settings and beyond current customer and competitors. They allow you to become aware of the part of the world you are not paying attention to.

When you are in the question, you will not be distracted by the viewpoints of people who choose to function from contextual reality. You will see discrepancies, such as changes that are outside the norms or outcomes that contradict each other. Leaders who are being functional with contextual reality are willing to wonder why something happened and then conceive of alternative or discontinuous responses. Remarkable innovators (Einstein), incredible avant-gardists and artists (Leonardo da Vinci), influential leaders (Socrates, John F. Kennedy, Golda Meir, Martin Luther King, Eleanor Roosevelt, Steve Jobs, etc.) do this naturally. These remarkable people have an astounding capacity for eliminating their preconceptions and seeing things through a fresh, unfiltered lens. This allows them to see the situation precisely and open-mindedly. Conversely, most of us are not able to see discrepancies and different possibilities with ease because we tend to get bogged down by following the norms, and aligning our business with conventional business models. Why? We want to please everyone and are always looking for where we fit, how we benefit, where we can win, and how to avoid losing.

Consciously Asking Non-contextual Questions

Consciously asking non-contextual questions has helped many organizations anticipate and prepare for threats and potential shifts in their environments. None of these possible threats may materialize, but it pays to be conscious and aware of their potentials. For example, to consider reality head on, during a strategic planning process in the late 1990s, the Enron Federal Credit Union mulled over an unimaginable scenario by asking: What would happen if Enron ceased to exist? They used non-contextual questions during scenario planning to direct more awareness and consideration toward the possibilities, probabilities, and risks. Rather than just focusing on its core relationships with Enron, the credit union expanded its membership and marketing efforts. Asking these non-contextual questions proved crucial to Enron Federal Credit Union's survival when the unthinkable did happen and Enron collapsed. It paid to be functional with this contextual reality.

Non-contextual questions such as the ones given below will give you an idea of how to get started.

- *What's possible for our organization?*

- *Can that be done in any other way?*

- *What other choices do we have?*

- *What would happen if we did that?*

- *What possibilities could this choice open up?*

- *What emerging technologies could change the game?*

- *What can we do about this?*

- *Could there be future changes or surprises that could harm or benefit us?*

- *What do I perceive that needs to be done that nobody else is attending to?*

- *What do I need to be aware of, to be effective in attending to it in a highly efficient and generative manner?*

- *If I couldn't do this the way we are currently doing it, how could I do it?*

- *What do I need to be aware of here?*

- *Where is everyone functioning from?*

- *What contribution can I be?*

- *What is this?*

- *What do I do with it?*

- *Can I change it?*

- *How can I change it?*

- *Where can I put my energy in that would change something?*

Let Contextual Reality Work For You.

Companies that operate with non-contextual awareness while being functional with contextual reality are more likely to thrive, more likely to be successful, and more likely to develop and launch innovative products and services. Being functional with contextual reality can generate billions of dollars in market value for the organization. For example, in the late 1990s, a flood of illegal music file sharing was occurring across the globe. By 2003, more than 2 billion illegal music files were being exchanged every month over the Internet. Music industry executives were understandably worried as music CD sales continued to decline in the face of downloading. As they fought to stop the knocking down of traditional music distribution and the annihilation of the physical CD market, the demand for digital music downloading continued to grow. Music industry executives refused to acknowledge what music customers required. They preferred it when things remained constant and stable.

Music industry executives were blinded by the status quo. They assumed things were pretty good the way they were and they desired that things remain just the way they were. They chose to fight global customer behavior rather than use where these people functioned from to their advantage. As this example shows, business status quo and dogmas are so deeply ingrained as to be almost invisible—and they are often fervently held as indisputable. The conventional music industry was bound by a consensual set of constraints that limited their ability to address new prospects and possibilities. They never questioned their beliefs. They never asked: Is this idea still true? Is it rewarding to maintain this point of view?

In contrast, Apple Inc. took on this challenge. They leaped over the music industry's preconceived notions and everyone else's best practices to conceive different possibilities. In 2001, they capitalized on this trend by launching the iTunes online music store, which provided legal, easy-to-use, flexible song downloads. Apple was being functional with contextual reality. They found new ways to operate beyond the bounds of music industry normalcy and conventional practices. They used their awareness of where music customers were functioning from to their strategic advantage. Customers have flocked to iTunes, and recording companies and artists are benefiting. Apple thinks differently about business. More often than not, it simply disregards conventional notions of business opportunities. Apple Inc's. approach to business strategy twines strategic awareness with flexibility, non-contextual awareness with discipline, and receptivity with accountability. It is the adroit combination of these counter-factors that makes Apple both uniquely innovative and generative from the edge of infinite possibilities.

Unlike so many other companies, Apple executives were being functional with contextual reality. They generated their business by perceiving a possibility that needed to be realized. They began with the idea that a legal online music store was possible. Then they set teams to work figuring out what it would take to make this happen. They were willing to be the energy, space, and consciousness required to generate a different result. Being functional with this reality is not done from a single intense focus; it is done from awareness of all things. Apple executives had an awareness of the big picture and an explicit insight of the situation at hand. They contributed to what was already in existence. Rather than fighting what already existed, they used it to generate something greater.

When leaders use awareness, they see the bigger picture; they are able to look at situations from a different place because they are aware they don't judge what they perceive. They ask non-contextual questions—and then they let contextual reality work for them. It requires their choice to be willing to be large enough to not be the effect of the thoughts, feelings, and emotions of other people. It also requires an unshakable trust in their ability to be aware of all possibilities, not just the ones they think they already know. In our view, these are the attributes Steve Jobs and the leaders at Apple bring to their work. They seem to generate their business from a sense of adventure rather than a default map. They seem to perceive, know, be, and receive with clarity that they have so many choices and they seem to have non-contextual awareness while effectively functioning with contextual reality. That's what makes Apple so very different from any others.

Operate Outside Contextual Reality

Steve Jobs, the founder and former CEO of Apple, was a great example of a leader who operated with non-contextual awareness as well as being functional with contextual reality. Steve Jobs was one of the first to see the vast business potential of the Internet. With the launch of iTunes in 2001, he began generating businesses that merged consumer products with the Web, which ultimately led to everything from the iPhone to the iCloud. At every turn, Steve Jobs took the road less travelled. He had an unshakeable courage and trust in his tenets, even though his initiatives and ventures confounded conventional practices, and often unleashed irregularity, mayhem, and chaos. Steve Jobs caused a stir in the record business by creating what was easily the most significant and major legal digital-music service on the market. The iTunes digital store has forever changed not only how music is sold and distributed, but also the way artists release and market songs and how they are bought and used by fans. Steve Jobs told *Fortune Magazine* "this will go down in history as a turning point for the music industry." The iTunes Music Store has rejuvenated the ailing music business because it is simple and user-friendly. Users can listen to a 30-second preview of any song and then, with one click, buy a high-quality audio copy for just 99 cents. There's no monthly subscription fee, and users have practically autonomous ownership of the music they download. The major music companies, by contrast, have tried to come up with legal alternatives but were unsuccessful. None of their schemes have taken off because they are too pricey and user-hostile. The ways record companies operate their business have been about how to be in context with this reality. They have always looked for where they fit, how they benefited, where they could win, and how they could avoid losing. They were so fearful about doing anything that might cannibalize CD sales, so they decided to "rent" music through the Internet. Users had to pay monthly subscription fees for songs from MusicNet and press play. Unfortunately, users could download MusicNet tunes to only one computer, and they disappeared if users didn't pay their bill. This contextual way of thinking may have protected the record companies from piracy, but it certainly didn't work for the users. Steve Jobs was able to generate unorthodox products and services because he wasn't a prisoner of contextual reality. He was willing to be different and willing to go on the journey nobody else would go on.

Apple succeeded because, in our view, Steve Jobs realized that to thrive and prosper in the crowded MP3 and mobile phone market, Apple must operate outside this contextual reality. The iPhone was not trying to compete with other mobile phones as a communication or business device. Instead, the iPhone is a combination of mobile phone, wide-screen iPod, camera, and a wireless touch-screen Internet communicator for Web browsing, with a remarkable array of applications for business and leisure, email and texting. Apple has created the first multipurpose mobile gadget.

Steve Jobs perceived things differently and functioned beyond current business models and constraints. He was a master of change since he didn't accept current realities and chose to perceive beyond them. He was a visionary and had a strong penchant for innovation. He enjoyed and was at his best when creating new and innovative products. He had an exceptional ability to envision things that did not yet exist and to inspire people to perceive and receive his vision. To envisage the ideas for iPhone, iTunes, and for other Apple products, he had to be willing to totally be, know, perceive, and receive outside this contextual reality and allow new possibilities to show up in his awareness. Another compelling aspect of Steve Jobs' success was that he was willing to act on the fringe, take risk, and never try to put himself in context with everything else. Underpinning Apple's remarkable approach is the consistency and the ingenuity of its products. Apple is not without its bugs and exploding batteries, but for thirty years it has innovated and redefined the way we use technology, communicate online, and consume, create, and share media.

Steve Jobs chose to go beyond competing to seize new possibilities, growth opportunities, and new profits. His willingness to venture from the known set him apart from other business leaders. He had an amazing ability to use where people function from to his advantage. The benefit of this ability shows up directly in Apple's bottom line. In the second quarter of 2009, Apple posted revenue of $8.16 billion and a net quarterly profit of $1.21 billion, or $1.33 per diluted share. Quarterly, iPhone units sold were 3.79 million, representing 123 percent unit growth over the same quarter a year ago. And now the new iPhone has been released, and its figures are surpassing the original iPhone.

In our view, Steve Jobs demonstrated that when we choose to be non-contextual awareness and to function with contextual reality, miracles occur.

Operating beyond contextual reality and being functional with contextual reality allowed Steve Jobs and the Apple executives to see business as an extraordinary adventure and to create their business anew in every moment.

It is about being indefinable and not creating the business based on fixed identity, industry definition, or past reference points. Every identity and definition is a limitation.

The rare pairing of contrarian leadership with big-picture vision was a Steve Jobs hallmark. He told students during a commencement address at Stanford in 2005. "Don't be trapped by dogma—which is living with the results of other people's thinking. Don't let the noise of others' opinions drown out your own inner voice. And most important, have the courage to follow your heart and intuition." His legacy cannot be ignored, especially by those who benefit from modern technology and those who value real honest-to-goodness design. He will be remembered as a business visionary for a very long time.

So, what can you learn from the experience of Steve Jobs as the CEO of Apple?

One: An unshakeable courage and trust in his tenets.

Steve Jobs knew what was important to him and Apple, and he let this be their compass bearing. He had an amazing ability to perceive the total picture, able to foresee strategic opportunities, and take astute and pragmatic action. He was willing to perceive, know, be, and receive the infinite possibilities that were available. He allowed new possibilities to show up. This is an unacknowledged asset of non-contextual awareness that few acquire. For most people this potency and power has been hidden and undeveloped. Steve Jobs had an uncanny ability to define the essential elements of anything—and ruthlessly cut everything else out. The result would be a long string of artistic masterpieces: the Apple logo, the Macintosh, the iPod, the iPhone, the iPad. Compare it to the typical hardware product like a Windows-based PC, usually loaded with features we don't need.

Two: Spontaneous, Flexible, Adaptive, Responsive.

Steve Jobs illustrates that nothing can stop us from leading, living, and truly being from the edge of infinite possibility, if we really want to have it. He was radically creative, and most importantly he knew when to say no. He was extremely disciplined about creativity, and he also encouraged wild and bold runaway thoughts that led to breakthroughs as much as they did dead-ends. According to Steve Jobs, "The trick is to know which is which." We have to go beyond traditional thinking about an industry, discover what the new opportunities are, and really choose from possibilities. The ability to operate beyond contextual reality means attaining a level of awareness where previously inconceivable things are available. "That was the essence of Jobs' unique genius—understanding that absence defines presence; that the only path to the great new things of the future was the merciless elimination of the good old things of the past," Jeff Yang writes in the *Wall Street Journal*.

Three: Defy the norms of conventional practice.

Steve Jobs was willing to go forth against a sea of adversity to build businesses that are generative and capable of continuous self-regeneration. He didn't define his business so it just fit the context of this reality. He was not limited by any ideas and was open to all possibilities; therefore he had a strategic advantage over everybody that was functioning from contextual reality. He demonstrated that when a leader functions from non-contextual awareness, he or she can employ contextual reality to work for them. Steve Jobs also described what it means to defy the norms of conventional practice, best summarized in his own words: "The system is that there is no system. That doesn't mean we don't have process. Apple is a very disciplined company, and we have great processes. But that's not what it's about. Process makes you more efficient. But innovation comes from people meeting up in the hallways or calling each other at 10:30 at night with a new idea, or because they realized something that shoots holes in how we've been thinking about a problem. It's ad hoc meetings of six people called by someone who thinks he has figured out the coolest new thing ever and who wants to know what other people think of his idea. And it comes from saying no to 1,000 things to make sure we don't get on the wrong track or try to do too much. We're always thinking about new markets we could enter, but it's only by saying no that you can concentrate on the things that are really important." – As quoted in "The Seed of Apple's Innovation" in *BusinessWeek* (October 12, 2004)

Four: Ability to go beyond competing and the willingness to seize new possibilities.

Steve Jobs was able to perceive and know the truth; others are misled by appearances that are based on this contextual reality. He wasn't bound by a collective unconscious viewpoint and a consensus restriction that limits other people's ability to perceive, know, be, and receive different possibilities. This is why he was able to operate beyond contextual reality as well as being functional with this contextual reality. Steve Jobs put forward that the success of an organization is the ability to think differently, and the willingness to seize new possibilities, best summarized in his own words:

Most companies lead with messages about what they sell, but that the great leaders and companies communicate why they do what they do. Everything Apple Inc. does, we believe in challenging the status quo. We believe in thinking differently. Apple challenges the status quo by making beautifully-designed, reliable products." "Look at the design of a lot of consumer products—they're really complicated surfaces. We tried to make something much more holistic and simple. When you first start off trying to solve a problem, the first solutions you come up with are very complex, and most people stop there. But if you keep going, and live with the problem and peel more layers of the onion off, you can often times arrive at some very elegant and simple solutions. Most people just don't put in the time or energy to get there. We believe that customers are smart, and want objects which are well thought through. Steve Jobs, on the design of the iPod, as quoted in Newsweek (October 14, 2006).

Being Unstoppable

Great innovation is nearly impossible if you remain blinded by the norms of conventional practice that are propped up by contextual reality. Great innovation requires transcending the contextual reality and the preconceived points of view, to instead operate from the edge of infinite possibilities. The truth is that business innovation is about being functional with this contextual reality and being willing to allow this reality to work for you.

When you function like that, you're unstoppable. Given the power of being functional with this contextual reality to deliver out-of-the-ordinary performance, it is odd that so few leaders possess a well-honed capacity to transcend the contextual reality and lead at the generative edge of infinite possibilities.

Can you imagine what your business would be like if you no longer lived by the rules of this reality? What would it be like to live at the generative edge of infinite possibilities and be open to life in such a way that celebration becomes your natural state of being? The full sense of being functional with this contextual reality comes only to the person who approaches every moment with a deep sense of adventure and curiosity, as well as generosity of spirit toward others.

To step into this space would be to move out of everything you ever thought was real, everything you thought was true, and everything you have been sold, told, or learned. When you move beyond that, a whole new universe opens up to you. It's just a choice. Truth is, there are not more than a handful of companies on the planet that have, like Apple, cultivated an ability to operate beyond contextual reality as well as being functional with this contextual reality. Many companies will choose not to make it so they can maintain their status quo, security, predictability, and the false identity they know based on the code of contextual reality.

It is important to be aware of and acknowledge that everyone has infinite potential to be functional with this contextual reality and to operate beyond contextual reality. Being functional with this contextual reality is about right here, right now. It is the moment you choose to be all that is possible. This is a choice you have to make. You have to make a demand of yourself: "No matter what it takes, no matter what it looks like, I am going down this path." You can ask: "What is it going to take to have that? What's it going to take to operate beyond contextual reality as well as being functional with this contextual reality?"

CHAPTER TEN

The Ability To Change And Transform On A Dime

The potency of life is the ability to be the catalyst for the change and transformation of all things and everyone. In life, if you are the catalyst, if you are the chemical that changes everything else then you are that thing that creates a reaction in the world to what you are being.
~ Gary Douglas

Over the next decade businesses will be challenged to change more than leaders can imagine. To meet the challenges of the next decade—and to take full advantage of the possibilities—they need to cultivate the ability to change and transform on a dime. Leaders who are flexible and able to change rise above obstacles. They live in the question and remain open to all possibilities so their organization can change and grow. They participate in an open exchange with their industry, community, environment, and the world, which enables them to employ what is available and what might be possible into the future to enhance their growth. Please recognize that everything in nature operates in this way. The ability to change and transform on a dime comes from the capacity to adapt as needed and to create flexible structures that are appropriate and suitable for that moment. Business leaders who cultivate the ability to change and transform themselves for immediate and sustainable growth are able to capture the relevant rewards.

Organizations ensnared in the business-as-usual paradigm tend to resist change and find it difficult to adapt to new developments. They tend to be devoted to infrastructure and invested in policy and procedure. They focus on reducing unpredictability, minimizing changeability, and improving efficiency. In other words, they venerate form, structure, significance, and linearity.

Form, Structure, Significance, and Linearity

Form and Structure.

Form is the shape or outline of something. It is also the way something is done or a conventional way of acting or behaving. For example, some organizations use Quality Management Systems (ISO 9001 etc.) as a justification to maintain existing systems without questioning what else is possible. This focus on form can stifle creativity and innovation.

Structure is the manner of organizing, building, or constructing something that makes sure everything runs in an orderly manner. For example, policies and procedures can also be used as innovation and creativity killers, depending on the point of view of the leaders. If they see the policies and procedures as fixed and immutable, then that is what they create. If they see them as guidelines and mechanisms to create a learning organization, then that also will occur.

Flexible leaders don't lock themselves into rigid forms and structures. They generate and arrange whatever forms best suit their present situation and remain open to changing them as the situation warrants. An example of one of the great flexible leaders is A.G. Lafley, Chairman and CEO of Procter & Gamble. Since taking charge in 2000, when Procter & Gamble was sinking under the weight of too many new products and organizational changes, Lafley has refocused on consumers and rejuvenated core businesses. P&G

once was known for innovating entirely on its own. But Lafley took the bold step of forcing P&G to partner with other companies—even rivals— in order to innovate. He boosted P&G's commitment to consumer input by going beyond focus groups to enter consumers' homes and the online worlds they visit. He de-emphasized traditional R&D spending in favor of product ideas culled from outside the company. For Lafley, that didn't mean poring over market research reports and lining up focus groups, which he frankly avoids. Instead, he visits dozens of everyday consumers each year, sitting down in their homes or walking with them through their local grocery store. A housekeeper from Venezuela tells him why she uses five different skin lotions for her feet, face, body, and hands. In Vietnam, a homemaker explains why she uses the competitor's laundry detergent. Lafley says he gets pearls of wisdom and awareness from customers he meets, almost always women. *"It's keeping you in touch with the qualitative side,"* he has been quoted as saying. Most chief executives, as Lafley has often observed, get too internally focused and neglect the importance of what's going on around them. Lafley took the traditional form and structure of market research and turned it on its head.

Unfortunately, many business people trained in traditional leadership paradigms have become convinced that they must have rigid forms and structures to ensure that everyone in the organization is focused on doing things in a consistent and predictable manner. The experience of Kodak (discussed in Chapter Two) illustrates just how devastating it can be to govern a company with rigid form and structure. The leaders at Kodak were so fixed in their ways that they couldn't take advantage of the industry's early warning signals of massive impending change in their industry due to the digital revolution.

Significance.

Something that is significant is considered to be meaningful, important, or consequential. Form and structure become significant when leaders believe that the forms and structures they have instituted are the only right way of doing things. They then allow form and structure to rule them and their organization. They believe that their way is the only way, and they concentrate their energy on proving that they are right. In organizations like these, form and structure become more important than the awareness, knowledge, and creativity of the people working in the organization. Take a moment to let that sink in. When you make something significant, you substitute your awareness for the idea that the thing is more important than your infinite awareness.

Form and structure and significance play out in all aspects of our lives and they dictate many of our major choices. For example, people have form, structure, and significance about the kind of work they're willing to do, the food they're willing to eat, and the kind of investments they're willing to make. Do these fixed positions limit them? Absolutely! The thing is, when you make something important, you are owned by it. You allow it to rule you. You are no longer able to freely perceive what is and lead from the edge of infinite possibility.

Linearity.

Linearity refers to a logical or analytical way of approaching issues that follows known information in a step-by-step progression. It's thinking in straight lines. Certainly a logical or analytical approach has its place in business, but when linear approaches dominate an organization, there is no room for creativity, insight, or intuition. Contextual awareness takes over and extinguishes the possibilities.

The Awareness Rut

When leaders strive for stability and predictability by imposing rigid form and structure, they constrict innovation, inhibit change, and create conditions that threaten an organization's survival. They corrupt people's ability to think and perceive. This creates an awareness rut where people tend to ignore information or data that doesn't fit the existing form and structure. Staffs have problems perceiving and receiving new ideas. They don't see other choices and other possibilities. The awareness rut poses particular problems when setting a strategy for businesses, because the strategy is often constrained by mindsets and viewpoints based on rigid forms. Organizations that have rigid form and structure easily degenerate into bureaucracy.

Several years ago, a forceful dedication to quality swept the global business arena. Many organizations developed a strategy that incorporated quality assurance standards to encourage their staff to continuously improve their work. The program was very successful in organizations that used a quality standard strategy as a source for reducing complexity and increasing high-quality products and services. Staff saw that they actually had a choice and the ability to generate better results.

The program was less successful in organizations that imposed quality standards on their business as a way of measuring performance, and assuring compliance and conformance to rigid plans. The rationale and justification for the rigid forms and structures was the apprehension that something could go wrong and the fear that everything would be lost. These organizations tended to waste a lot of time on process, form and structure, and people became frustrated when the desired outcomes were not accomplished.

Organizations that impose quality standards on their business as a tool for measurement and judgment have a commitment to contextual reality. Everything is about fitting in, benefiting, winning, and not losing. These organizations tend to lock their staff into positions where they feel they have no choice. They rob their staff of the chance to grow by enforcing a rigid, closely supervised program that drives them to improve their performance. At some point, creative juices stop flowing and innovation dries up. As these organizations continue to impose control, people become less and less effective.

True innovators are never bound by form, structure, significance, and linearity. Many leading companies such as Berkshire Hathaway, Starbucks, and Google promote a philosophy of leading without control, force, and effort. They encourage and inspire their employees to bring all of their capabilities to work every day. If you want unbounded contributions from your staff, you must be willing to let go of rigid plans, strict policies, mandatory procedures, and comprehensive assessments. Google Chairman and CEO Eric E. Schmidt embodies the ideal innovative business leader in the digital age. Google obsesses about innovation. It is the key to their plans for continued growth. Schmidt believes innovation only comes from the luxury of being able to think of a new idea and pursue it. Thinking of new ideas requires freedom from thinking about other obligations. With this is mind Google has their engineers spend about 20 percent of their time, or a day a week, pursuing new ideas in small and undirected technology teams. Schmidt believes thinking outside the box requires the absence of managerial oversight. Schmidt also uses acquisitions of small companies to supplement their in-house innovation. In his words, "small companies often have the great new ideas". Schmidt believes in the wisdom of crowds and runs Google by consensus. In order to make this work, Schmidt recommends using strict deadlines to create a crisis (in the absence of real crises) and to encourage dissent and disagreement. He seeks out people who are silent during meetings hoping to encourage those who disagree to speak out. Only by doing this can all the important information be released and the right decision made. Since innovation is the key to Google's success, everything Schmidt does revolves around creating more innovation. Without it, Schmidt believes there is nothing to prevent another company from overtaking Google as the king of digital information. Innovation is systematically encouraged at Google at all levels throughout the organization, including management.

Form and structure aren't necessarily bad, as long as they are not made significant. They must be recognized for what they are—and what they aren't. It is vital to become aware of any fixed positions you have created and imposed on yourself and your organization. Without this awareness, it is easy to fall prey to the awareness rut and the manner in which it dictates your habitual behaviors. Ask yourself:

- *How many reference points do I have that hold me back?*

- *What are the defined limitations of my life?*

- *To what extent do I and my business operate according to outmoded practices, policies, and systems?*

- *How much form, structure, and significance have I aligned and agreed with that stops me from expanding my awareness?*

- *What limiting beliefs do I function from in life that are creating my reality?*

- *How many systems and structures do I use in my life and my organization because things have always been done that way?*

Your Job as a Leader

Some might argue that to create a successful business, leaders must set standards and keep their staff from running amok or becoming disorderly and undisciplined. That may be true in some cases, but when you set a rigid standard based on what's right vs. wrong, you have done your business and everyone in it a disservice.

We are not suggesting that organizations should function in an unconscious environment of "whatever." Nor are we suggesting that business should not aim to deliver exceptional quality to agreed-upon standards. However, standards should not be used as a context for measuring people's behavior or performance. The willingness to change doesn't mean steering an organization with no strategic vision or clarity of direction. On the contrary, leaders must generate a conscious strategy—one that has substantial flexibility and suppleness built into it. Strategy should be developed and continuously reaffirmed. Leaders should also continuously ask: "What have we missed?" and make changes when required.

Unfortunately, people who function based on contextual reality often misidentify and misapply the notion of what a standard is. They tend to use standards to judge people—and they do so continuously. They do not allow the free flow of information regarding performance, financials, strategy, and other areas. They actively cultivate a climate of fear and punishment through systematized organizational disincentives, and they have such rigid mindsets and standards that no other possibilities are allowed. They are focused on systems and processes that create order and are not open to change.

The attachment to standards tends to blind leaders to the need for change. They attempt to hang onto their security and resist what does not fit their standard. They resist other possibilities that are being offered because they want to maintain the rightness of their point of view. In being right, they refuse to be different. Their insistence on being right destroys the possibility of success. It blocks them from making wise choices and taking effective action.

When we introduce this notion in our workshop presentations, someone from the audience invariably asks, "Isn't it our job as leaders to direct and control our workforce? If we don't have control, would this not create chaos in our organization?" The frequency with which this question is asked has led us to realize that most people misidentify and misapply the meaning of leadership. In our view there's a difference between someone who takes charge and someone who is a leader. The truth is you can't lead people unless they are willing to follow you.

Please recognize that if you persistently use rigid standards to assess, measure, and judge your employees, you are likely to suppress the talents and abilities of the very people on whom you must rely to deliver your business vision. Many tough-minded leaders sneer at this notion because they believe that good leaders must have the right answer and take decisive action. They have a great fondness for the old command-and-control model of leading a business. Many of these people have assumed that a successful leader must be seen to be firm and uncompromising. How do you see your job as a leader? Think about the management processes in your company.

- *Do you inspire people to go above and beyond?*

- *Do you motivate them to do their best?*

- *Are your people sincerely willing to do more than what is normally expected to help the organization succeed?*

- *Do they have the freedom to choose the way they do their job or execute their responsibilities?*

- *Do you give your people the chance to be a contribution, to make a difference, and exercise their talents and abilities?*

- *Do you inspire them to bring all of their capabilities to work every day?*

If your answers to these questions are *not really* or *not very much*, are you aware that you are unlikely motivating people to be fully engaged in their work? If this is the case, you're operating at a real strategic disadvantage. The more you shackle people through rigid control, micromanagement, or the constraints of policy, rigid procedures, and processes, the less engaged and inspired they will be about their work.

Are You Micromanaging Your Staff?

Micromanagement is a surefire way not to have joy in your life. Micromanaging is like planting a little seed. You poke it in the ground, water it and cover it up. Then you go back a day later, pull the seed out and ask, "Are you growing yet? No? Hey, what's going on? I thought you were going to grow." Then you put it back in the ground, water it, come back the next day and pull it out again. After about ten days of this, the seed is dead.
~ Gary Douglas

Micromanagement tends to squelch originality and awareness. It teaches your staff to become risk averse. An overemphasis on standardization and micromanagement deters people from engendering out-of-scope opportunities and encourages them to hold back on the exploration for new strategic advantage. You are micromanaging when you:

- *See leadership as taking charge of your organization*

- *Believe you need to have all the answers*

- *Think it's your job to tell others what to do*

- *Expect your staff do what you want them to do when you want them to do it*

- *Look over everyone's shoulders*

- *Tell people how to conduct themselves*

When you micromanage, you are asking for problems. It is sheer absurdity for leaders to think they can competently micromanage their entire business themselves. If you find yourself (like many conventional business leaders) telling yourself, "I gotta take care of this issue, this problem, or this person. I gotta to do this and I gotta do that," you are probably micromanaging your staff. This isn't your job as a leader.

Your job is to hire the right people for the job and surround yourself with people who are competent and skillful—and then to allow them to do what they are good at without your interference. Individual contributions tend to be inhibited in organizations that have rigid policy, procedure, and micromanagement processes. If not curbed, the tendency to micromanage can metastasize into an unwholesome fondness for conformity, where novel ideas and new possibilities are seen as dangerous deviations from standard operating procedure.

Leading Without Control, Force, and Effort

Warren Buffett, one of the wealthiest people on the planet, is a highly respected business leader who illustrates what it is like to achieve amazingly spectacular success by leading without control, force, and effort. Warren owns more than eighty-eight diverse businesses. To ensure that his businesses are proficiently operated, he hands over authority to his leadership team. He entrusts all of his CEOs to make decisions without having to consult him or get his approval. Contrary to what many other people think, Warren believes that leadership is not about controlling or micromanaging. It is not about having power over people. He perceives that his generative power comes from his ability to make other people powerful. What makes Warren Buffet a great leader is his ability to encourage people to know that they know. He is renowned for asking questions that inspire people to come up with their own ideas for doing things. He illustrates a remarkable inquisitiveness and curiosity, and he enjoys speaking with people on the front lines. Warren Buffett's view of leadership demonstrates that for a business to flourish and grow, leaders must inspire their people to greatness at their job. His leadership philosophy has allowed him to expand the operational annual net income of Berkshire Hathaway from $18 per share in 1979 to $118,000 per share in 2010, with little sign of abating!

Warren Buffett demonstrates that it is truly possible to achieve great wealth and success without control, force, and effort while doing what you love. Publicly, Warren Buffett has stated that he perceives money as a by-product of something he loves to do. For him money is not an end in itself. He has said that when he gets up in the morning he goes to his pleasure dome—his office. According to Warren, not doing what we love in the name of greed is a gloomy way to live. He has said many people do what they do just for the money, and to him, that's not a good reason to do anything. Loving what you do is the fuel you need to keep reaching for what you know is possible and become a generative element in the world. If you're doing something you love, you're more likely to put your all into it, and that generally results in making money.

The key to Warren's success is that he values the magic that he is as the source of his life, and not the money he can generate. He has achieved his wealth by being aware of nascent companies that were likely to blossom and prosper in the future. He follows his awareness—and not the crowd. He has an amazing ability to stand alone when the winds of popular opinion are against him. He buys stocks when everyone else is anxious and fearful, and he sells when everyone else is voracious and acquisitive. He has spent his life going against the herd. According to Warren, "You're neither right nor wrong because other people agree with you. You're right because your facts are right and your reasoning is right—and that's the only thing that makes you right. And if your facts and reasoning are right, you don't have to worry about anybody else."

He has a history of standing alone that dates back to the early days of his investing career. Most of the stocks he owns were purchased when no one wanted them. If he had followed the crowd or followed the direction from Wall Street, he would have missed out on some of his greatest investments. If he can't find an investment that's selling at an attractive price, he'll wait and wait. In the late 1960s, he wrote to his investing partners that he couldn't find any investments that he understood at attractive prices. He waited until 1973 when the stock market collapsed and some of the best companies were selling at bargain prices. He believes that if he doesn't empathize with a business venture, it's not worth looking at, even if the business is popular at the time. He says, "Pick the wrong company at the right price and you lose. Pick the right company at the wrong price and you lose. You have to pick the right company at the right price and to do that you have to wait and wait patiently." He trusts in himself and in his awareness, no matter what anyone else thinks.

Warren Buffett is incontestably the greatest investor of all time. The impetus of his life is unquestionably generating beyond the bottom line. In our view, Warren Buffett truly functions on the edge of possibility and makes the most of his unique talents and abilities for the greatest benefit. (What shows this?) Money isn't what drives him even though he is making a lot. What drives him is a love of what he does.

Reflection

Are you spending your time and energy examining and monitoring the context of your business from a fixed vantage point?

Are you looking at circumstances and conditions through a narrow company or industry lens that is based on the past?

Letting Go of the Status Quo

Research conducted by The Carnegie Institute of Technology has revealed that 85 percent of a leader's success in business is due to his or her way of being and ability to relate with people effectively. Only 15 percent of a leader's success is due to technical training and experience, brainpower, or skill on the job. Unfortunately most standard leadership training programs focus exclusively on these skills. As a result, these programs develop controllers rather than leaders. They teach leaders to sustain a controlled structure in which staff follow specified directives and perform them efficiently in the approved manner.

In our experience, the most dysfunctional leaders are those who seek to preserve the status quo. They spend their time trying to control and make good soldiers of the team. Business leaders who seek to preserve the status quo facilitate an unconscious culture, or worse, an anti-conscious culture of fear and risk aversion. Their attitude impairs their organization's ability to change and transform with ease, and they are not able to handle the business requirements and the world as it changes constantly around them.

We encourage you to abandon points of view that have always been at the heart of traditional thinking. Let go of the constant need to control. Stop putting yourself and your business in context with everything else. These recommendations may be at odds with your normal understanding of how businesses are supposed to operate, but contrary to what you may think, real leadership is not about controlling or managing. It is not about having power over people. Control is an illusion, anyway, and the attempt to control people and situations generates never-ending predicaments and misconduct in the workplace. When leaders engage in tightly controlling behavior in an attempt to make sure that everything goes the way they want it to go, they often generate rigidity in thought and action in themselves as well as their staff.

What Does It Mean to Be Out of Control?

From the viewpoint of strategic awareness perspective, true power comes from the willingness to be out of control, out of definition, out of limitation, and out of form, structure, and significance.

Being out of control is not being uncontrolled. It is not being drunk, disorderly, disruptive, or unruly. Being out of control is about not letting the controls of other people's points of view, judgments, and decisions be the controlling factor in your life. It is about knowing what is right for you. It takes initiative, fortitude, and determination to break out of the control of contextual reality and into the realm of infinite possibility.

In the business arena, being out of control is about releasing your business from the accepted boundaries that define how you should operate and how you must compete. Being out of control is taking back the places where you have given away parts of your life to other people's judgments and points of view. To be out of control is to no longer be the effect of the way others do things—and instead to be the contribution *you* can be.

We have noticed that whenever we are willing to let go of control and receive everything without judgment, we find ourselves in a powerful position of choice. If you have to control everything to lead your staff to make things happen and to make your organization successful, how much energy does that require of you? And if you are busy controlling everything, how much does that limit what you can create, innovate, and what you can achieve? It limits you a great deal!

Poor decisions are often made when leadership teams that believe they need to control outcomes dominate an organization. When you and your leadership team are able to let go of the need to control and are willing to be out of control, you will easily move into generating no-more-business-as-usual with a much greater level of efficiency and productivity.

Being out of definition is about being free from the definitions and limitations other people impose on you. Their definitions exist—and you are aware of them—but you operate outside of them. You are not defined by other people's expectations and beliefs about what you should be. Definition is always limitation. Most of us keep trying to define ourselves and our business by how much money we have or don't have. What our position is or what our position isn't. What we are trying to create or what we are not trying to create. What we are capable of creating or what we are incapable of creating. Those are all definitions. Every definition you have of you or your business creates a different set of rules and roles that you have to play. Being out of definition is about being indefinable, and not creating your life or your business based on identity, definition, or past reference points. Every identity and definition is a limitation, anything you value most in this reality becomes a trap which is a limitation for you. When you create your business from an identity, you create from a limited point of view, since each identity is a limitation. Access Consciousness is a good example of a business that demonstrates what it is like to be out of definition as a business. Access Consciousness doesn't really fit into a definition easily. Access is about facilitating consciousness and awareness and our knowing. The target of Access is to empower people to access what they know, not to tell them what to do. It's not a structured organization with an office and there isn't a building with a sign over the door saying Access Consciousness Centre. It doesn't have a mission statement or a defined set of goals and purposes from which it functions. Gary Douglas, the founder of Access Consciousness, describes it as an applied philosophy for life. However, a key difference of Access Consciousness from other philosophies is that Access is organic, constantly changing, and invites contribution from everyone who participates in it. Gary Douglas thrives on uncertainty, without form, structure, and significance. The key difference between traditional business leaders and Gary Douglas is that traditional business leaders often seek to establish limits, whereas Gary will look beyond them. Garry leads the business by allowing Access to be in a constant state of creating itself new, moment to moment, instead of maintaining its identity. What this means is the Access Consciousness business doesn't run by the rules of this reality, but operates at the creative edge of this reality. Gary is famous for hiring great people, and then he totally gives them the reins and lets them run with it. He never tries to control every task, every event, everything including the people involved. Instead he lets them set their own targets and standards. Gary allows all of his employees complete control over their jobs, however, he is always there to support them when they need him. When Gary looks for people to work for him, he looks for people who are willing to become conscious leaders in their own lives as well as in his business. Once Gary finds the people who have the right skills to do the job he then inspires and facilitates them to embody and be the greatness of whom they truly are. He then becomes a contribution to the consciousness of his business, his staff, and his clients by recognizing what will create the greatest change, and facilitating that. With this kind of leadership, Gary and his team are capable together of generating unlimited possibilities, and his business has grown exponentially.

Being out of limitation simply means that you do not operate within the limitations that others create for you and for themselves in business. Others will always define the limitations of you by what they are willing to have in their life. If you align and agree with them, by wanting them to see you or to validate you, you define you by the limitations they have put on you. To become out of limitation you have to become aware of where you are functioning from that is creating limitation in your business and in your life. For anything to be creating a limitation in your life you have to have either aligned and agreed with it or resisted and reacted to it. Clearing this will give you space for choice. Once you are choosing to be out of limitation, you have to be willing to step outside the box of limitation you have created your life as and you must not look to past experience as the source of what you will create in the future. When you are really willing to have the largeness of your life, you would be out of limitation. You start to live in the moment. Being out of limitation is truly possible and it doesn't have to occur according to the rules, the regulations, and the restrictions of this reality. You have to value you enough to be willing to be out of limitation. When you do, it's amazing how you become the inspiration to a totally different possibility and a totally different world. Richard Branson, a flamboyant British entrepreneur with a seemingly insatiable appetite for starting new businesses, demonstrates what it looks like to be out of limitation. Richard Branson is known as the king of the publicity stunt. In 1998, Branson drove a vintage Sherman tank down New York's Fifth Avenue to introduce Virgin Cola to the United States. According to website entrepreneur.com, the "adventure capitalist" then fired a cannon at the Coca-Cola sign. In October 2007, Branson set out to perform a bungee-meets-abseiling stunt to promote his new Virgin America domestic airline. Sporting a tuxedo, Branson climbed Las Vegas' The Palms Hotel before jumping off its roof. Besides being the king of the publicity stunt, he is also a phenomenally brilliant business tycoon. He has built the Virgin

Group into an international conglomerate of some 350 companies, many of them still tiny but all of them combining for more than $8 billion a year in sales. Richard Branson has been tagged as a "transformational leader" in the management lexicon, with his maverick strategies and his stress on the Virgin Group as an organization driven on informality and information, one that is bottom-heavy rather than strangled by top-level management. He has created one of the most recognizable brands in the world. In Britain where he focuses much of his attention, Branson has managed to "Virginize" a very wide range of products and services. The variety of businesses he controls is as vast as the geographical coverage the brand has, with businesses located throughout The United Kingdom, the United States of America, Australia, Canada, Asian, Europe, and South Africa. He is continuously seeking new business opportunities and loves a good challenge, especially when he enters a market that is dominated by a few major players. He does not play by the limitations that others seek to place on him.

Being out of form, structure, and significance is not being undisciplined, boisterous, crazy, wild, or lawless. It's not being bound by rigid forms and structures that others have deemed highly important and significant. It's being agile, responsive, and innovative. Ram Charan, one of the world's most renowned management consultants and authors, demonstrated what it looks like to be out of form, structure, and significance. Ram Charan chooses to live nowhere and go everywhere in his quest to help businesses solve their thorniest conundrums. He does not own a home, or even rent one. He has no nuclear family or significant material possessions, and he has his assistants FedEx his clean clothes to him. He is in perpetual motion, travelling globally, working for the largest and most powerful companies seven days a week, 365 days a year. He has become an indispensable right-hand man for hundreds of top managers. He helps demolish organizational silos or persuade entrenched executives to change their points of view. What makes Ram Charan so different from other consultants is that most consultants tell their clients what they want to hear. Ram Charan doesn't! He doesn't reinforce his clients' preconceived notions. Rather, he surrenders his own ego, asks lots of questions, and ultimately facilitates the executive to claim, own, and acknowledge his or her own awareness and knowing.

According to *Fast Company Magazine* (February 1, 2004), Ram Charan has been considered such an asset, in fact, that many of his clients are willing to do something that's awfully rare in the executive suite: to publicly acknowledge a consultant and give him the credit for helping them change their companies. "Ram will take an idea and make it better," says John C. Hodgson, executive vice president at DuPont, which has been working with Charan in different capacities for close to 15 years. "I use him as a sounding board. I value his thinking, his creativity, and his unbiased view of the world." Probing, questioning, and digging into the psyches of others is Charan's most successful technique. He has an awareness of what he would like to generate in the world energetically, and he carries the awareness of that energy with him no matter where he goes and no matter what he does. There is no form, structure, or significance in his work, just questions.

Without a doubt, the meticulous application of form and structure, such as standardization, policy, and procedure can lead to manufacturing efficiency, reliability, and high quality. Yet if the target is to generate business from the edge of infinite possibility, rigid form and structure can be restrictive and often toxic. Rigid form and structure don't produce superior performance. Standardization, policy, and procedure, for all their benefits, tend to limit innovation and prevent the organization from perceiving new and different possibilities. The more form and structure become significant in the organization, the less flexible and resilient the organization will be.

Create Forms and Structures That Move With Change

In our view, if an organization wishes to thrive, nothing in it can be based on fixed or unchangeable forms and structures. However, we are not advocating undisciplined business practices. We're not suggesting that form and structure are useless or of no value. A company without form and structure would soon plunge into disarray and mayhem. Instead we are advocating form and structure that moves with change. We suggest you institute forms and structures that are flexible and adaptive and that *enable* rather than *constrain*. What if it was truly possible to have flexible form and structure without losing substance and effectiveness? This is possible if leaders are willing to see that being out of limitation, out of definition, out of form, structure, and significance are ways of removing the typical organizational barriers to personal ingenuity and innovation. They unshackle people from the hypnotic power of contextual mindset.

To be out of form, structure, and significance requires you to become aware of the boundaries and restrictions that confine your behavior (as well as the behavior of your staff) and then deliberately let those boundaries and restrictions go or step beyond them. This is not about breaking the rules. It is about renouncing the significance conventions, rules, and regulations in general, and most especially those which do not contribute to your success. It is about finding more generative, dynamic, and flexible ways of being. To wrap you mind around these new ways of being requires having a shift of perspective and viewpoint. How do we break the cycle of significance? It's not a matter of exerting heroic will power. All that's required is the use of a simple discipline.

First you must acknowledge that you create limitation for yourself and your business with any points of view that you see as being enormously significant and indispensable. You must acknowledge that you choose to have your points of view and you also choose to attach significance to them.

Second you have to be willing to give up the things that you think are valuable and significant. You have to get to the point where you stop making anything significant. When you are making anything significant you give up access to all the awareness you could have other than that thing you have made significant.

What would it take for you to be in interesting point of view about everything? When everything is just an interesting point of view, you start to create choice in your life. You don't have choice otherwise.

Willing to Operate Outside the Box

Chef Heston Blumenthal, the British experimental chef and culinary wizard, is a well-known example of someone who has chosen to be out of control, out of definition, out of limitation, and out of form, structure, and significance with his business. He is not attached to culinary conventions or past reference points and seems always willing to take risks and destroy and un-create old systems, structures, and routines in favor of new ones.

Heston is able to generate an unorthodox business because he doesn't let the controls of other people's points of view, realties, judgments, and decisions be the controlling factor in his life. For Heston, it's not about breaking the rules—it's about throwing out the notion of rules altogether. He doesn't do contextual reality with his cooking. Two of his more well-known creations are bacon and egg ice cream and snail porridge, which he says, "may seem like a bizarre combination, but it is totally delicious to eat. You just have to get over the name."

He is an advocate of novel multisensory-drive cooking: He focuses on the sounds, the visuals, the smells, and, of course, the tastes and the flavors of the food he prepares. He constantly seeks out new ways to harmoniously stimulate all of the senses during the eating experience, orchestrating a succession of bursts of flavor in a dish or using smell to generate emotion or headphones to amplify the dimension of sound, such as the "crunch" of certain foods.

Heston has a vision of changing the way people experience food. He has opened his own research and development kitchen to research the molecular compounds of dishes, to bring about a greater understanding of taste and flavor. It could be said that he is influential, inspirational, and has transformed the way people think about what is possible, feasible, and attainable. So, what can we learn from the experience of Chef Heston Blumenthal?

One: Generate business by doing what you love.

Heston made it his priority to discover what he loved to do. Inventing extraordinary gastronomic creations is something that nourishes and fulfills him and at the same time allows him to generate huge amounts of money. He has pride in who he is and what he creates. He is willing to let people experience what he has created and have their own point of view and judgment about it. Heston is aware of who he is, what he is in love with, and what he wishes to accomplish, all of which gives him his extraordinary position in the world.

Two: Be willing to be out of the limitation, out of form, structure, and significance.

Heston has achieved astronomical success during the time of economic downturn because he has been willing to operate outside of the box. He has a fluid, flexible, and adaptive mindset that has allowed him to re-invent cooking. He has generated a remarkable business because he pushes the envelope and operates beyond the limitations of this contextual reality.

Three: Search for new experiences and new ways of doing things.

Instead of looking to compete within contextual reality, Heston has chosen to reconstruct market realities to go beyond the limitation of contextual reality. He recognizes that the culinary business arena is in perpetual motion and full of unlimited possibilities. His company has broken out conventional ways of doing things and presented us with possibilities we had not considered.

Reflection

Have you ever asked yourself and your leadership team:

How flexible and resilient is our business paradigm?

Must we be bound by the limitations of the form and structure of our standardizations, policies, and procedures?

Would it be possible for our organization to let go of the commitment to contextual reality?

These are essential questions for every leader who would like to lead from the edge of infinite possibilities. If you are up against deeply entrenched beliefs ask:

> **So what is it I am not willing to let go of, absolutely unwilling to let go of, that if I let go of it, would disconnect me from contextual mindsets?**

> **Is this belief true simply because we have made it real and true?**

If you are up against some rigid form, structure, and significance, it may be helpful to ask:

> **What's the value of holding on to this form, structure, and significance?**

> **Whose interest and benefit do they serve?**

In our work with business leaders around the world, we've had the opportunity to observe many organizations and the people who lead them. The most dynamic, effective, and generative leaders we've seen are those who embrace change. They are willing to give up fixed expectations and predetermined outcomes and change and transform on a dime. The sooner you start to release your organization from its legacy of business-as-usual mindsets, the sooner your business will begin to function from the edge of infinite possibilities.

CHAPTER ELEVEN

The Magic of Strategic Awareness

There is no fit, benefit, win, or lose possible when you are being energy, space, and consciousness. There is only question, choice, possibility, and contribution.
~ Gary Douglas

In our work with countless organizations around the world, we have discovered that the awareness of leaders has a profound effect on the ability of an organization to perform effectively. We have further observed that aware leaders are able to engender a thriving business when they choose to embody strategic awareness and prosperity consciousness. However, these qualities are missing in most business leaders. The lack of strategic awareness and prosperity consciousness explain why so many people are merely surviving and why so many business superstars wind up derailed, or even worse, end up in jail.

In today's environment of global financial crises, global warming, globalization, loss of local autonomy, and other issues, the lack of strategic awareness is a liability that organizations can no longer afford. Today leaders are required to consciously deal with not just the speed of change but also with complexity, chaos, uncertainty, and paradox. Detecting changes in the external environment on a continual basis and knowing what these changes mean to your business, is what we call true strategic awareness. It takes robust strategic awareness to effectively deal with the complexity and decipher the ambiguity to identify the trends and the new arrangements that are emerging. It is this robust strategic awareness that allows you to perceive and know where the world is going so that you can put a strategy in place to handle the impending hazards and the potential opportunities.

The future arises from a constant stream of actions, choices, decisions, and strategies that have to be made in the present with as much conscious awareness, foresight, skill, astuteness, and wisdom possible. Leaders cannot take shifts in stride if they become attached to a fixed strategic direction or predetermined outcome. Without strategic awareness, leaders may be unaware of new opportunities or unable to appropriately perceive critical threats. Leaders who lack strategic awareness become derailed and get discarded sooner, while the injury and dysfunction that they have set in motion can be devastating for a business.

So, What Exactly Is Being Strategic?

What do the terms *business strategy* or *strategic planning* mean to you? Strategic planning is often misidentified as a bothersome operational initiative that is done because the CEO or board requires it, so everyone can then say, "We have a strategic plan." Many leaders find creating a business strategy to be a difficult and mysterious process that yields unsatisfactory results. Simply calling something a strategic plan or a strategic initiative doesn't make it one. In fact, most strategic plans aren't truly strategic. They often consist of high-level ideas that are based on past experience.

Some organizations feel the need to have a strategic plan but find the process of proper strategic planning too costly, so they take shortcuts and create a plan so flawed and destructive that it is worse than not having one at all. Other organizations create strategic plans that are vague wish lists that are not measurable and never get reviewed. Still other organizations labor over documents that are developed over a six-month period, by which time everyone in the organization is so tired of the so-called planning process that they want nothing more than to bury the resulting document.

Our view is that being strategic means being clear about the organization's vision and mission, and being aware of its resources, and then incorporating this clarity and awareness into a state of conscious responsiveness to a dynamic, rapidly-changing business environment. Strategy is simply an agreed-upon course of action that an organization will take to achieve its vision and mission. It is a set of directions or a plan that will achieve the organization's vision and mission. Each of these "directions" is typically called strategies.

And What Is Strategic Awareness?

Strategic awareness places equal emphasis on both *strategy* and *awareness*. Strategic awareness is the process of fusing awareness to strategy and incorporating real-world knowledge of industry, global trends, and possible futures. It is the process of accessing non-analytic data and incorporating awareness or inner knowing into the strategic decision-making process.

Strategy and awareness are each essential to superior performance, which is the prime target of any enterprise. However, *strategy* and *awareness* work in very different ways. Awareness without strategy often results in leaders becoming mesmerized by the realm of potential possibility. They bounce from one idea to the next without any plan or strategy for carrying ideas through into physical reality. Awareness of the possibilities is important, but it's not enough. You have to be able to bring the ideas into the world—and a sound strategy allows you to do this. Have you met people who talk on and on about their visions and aspirations, yet never create anything? A bunch of amazing ideas without robust strategy will not make a person a successful business mogul. In fact, many notorious big-business failures have stemmed from feeble or faulty strategies. In their book *Billion Dollar Lessons*, Paul Carroll and Chunka Mui point out that many big business failures could have been avoided if companies had been more strategically aware of potential pitfalls. It takes generative energy, will power, fortitude, *and strategy* to transform awareness into physical reality.

On the other side, being *strategic* without *awareness* means focusing on how to improve or enhance the organization's current capacity or situation, while skipping the question, "What else is possible?" Without awareness, leaders easily become blind to changes and developments that the existing strategy has not taken into account. The organization focuses exclusively on their strategy. Leaders are not aware of the changes that are occurring in the world around them. Other possibilities are not recognized: The existing strategy becomes the "right" way to do things. Being strategic without awareness results in a cognitive bias that is prone to confirm evidence that is *believed* to be true.

So, neither awareness nor strategy alone is enough. But when awareness meets strategy, it has potential to change the world. Steve Jobs is a good example of what it means to embody strategic awareness. In our view, his phenomenal success is due to his brilliant capacity for marrying awareness with robust strategies. Every innovative product at Apple started with Steve Jobs' intensity of awareness of new possibilities—and a heavy dose of creative strategies that make the possibilities a reality. Not one of Steve Jobs' ideas would have stood a chance of becoming an innovative product had he not been able to operate from strategic awareness.

At the start of the new millennium, Steve Jobs became aware of the power of the digital technology revolution to evolve PC capability to the next level. He saw beyond the horizon and perceived that the PC was on the threshold of entering the age of the digital lifestyle. He then generated strategies to turn the Mac into a digital hub. As part of this strategy, Apple developed the iLife software program, which allows people to edit video (iMovie), create podcasts (GarageBand), organize photos (iPhoto) and more. The digital hub strategy has allowed Apple to prosper and thrive beyond anyone's imagination.

Strategic awareness is not a new concept. However, it has been discounted, ignored, and overlooked by conventional business people because it works in ways that are mysterious to their linear analytic minds. Importantly, strategic awareness defies one of the most commonly accepted doctrines of traditional business models—the need to operate from competitive advantage. One of the important elements of strategic awareness is prosperity consciousness. Prosperity consciousness has nothing to do with what you have. It has everything to do with who you choose to be. It is a knowing that the universe is an abundant place, and that there are truly infinite possibilities. If you choose to be prosperous and to be prosperity consciousness, then you can be. If you choose to be unconscious and to live in the scarcity paradigm, then you create your life based on that. It's your choice! However, most people function from the scarcity paradigm, where they believe there is not enough of anything (therefore they must get it before others do or miss out), where everything is hard and getting harder (so why should they even try, after all, it is so hard!), and where that's just the way it is, there is nothing that can be done about it (that's just the way the market is, the economy, our sector, etc.).

Prosperity consciousness, however, allows business leaders to focus on possibilities instead of profit. Organizations that function from prosperity consciousness and think globally position themselves for immediate and sustainable growth. By looking through the lens of prosperity consciousness, they can take advantage of new opportunities before others who are stuck in the old scarcity paradigm.

Today's leaders are required to consciously deal with not just the speed of change but also with complexity, chaos, uncertainty, and paradox. Detecting changes in the external environment on a constant basis and understanding what these changes mean to one's business is another element of strategic awareness. It takes robust strategic awareness to effectively deal with complexity and identify new trends and developments as they emerge. Strategic awareness allows you to perceive and know where the world is going so that you can put a strategy in place to handle impending hazards and seize potential opportunities. The sub-prime-triggered financial crisis of 2008 is a recent example of how traditional strategies failed to take into account the swiftness of change and the way in which venerable institutions (for example, Lehman Brothers) could falter when they were unable to perceive and deal with massive change. The derailment of many business executives illustrates the anti-conscious and unconscious choices people make without the foundation of strategic awareness and prosperity consciousness. Worldly power without strategic awareness and prosperity consciousness is the downfall of leadership.

What Sets Strategically Aware Leaders Apart?

Strategically aware leaders have four primary attributes that set them apart from others: expanded non-contextual awareness, powerful vision, the ability to extrapolate (the ability to project known information in order to infer something about the unknown), and the desire to be a contribution and serve the greater needs of society.

1. Expanded Non-Contextual Awareness

Strategic awareness begins with non-contextual awareness, which we define as the ability to know without the use of rational thought processes or direct cognition. It is the capacity to know without words and to perceive the truth without explanation, cognitive interpretation, reasoning, or justification. Non-contextual awareness, which we have discussed at length in Chapter Six, is the key to perceiving and receiving unlimited possibilities and seizing new opportunities.

2. Powerful Vision

The second element of strategic awareness is powerful vision. Strategic awareness is not a cognitive, analytical observation of what already exists. It focuses on what matters to an organization: Its vision and the impact it wishes to have on the community it serves. Strategic awareness allows leaders to become consciously aware of what is possible for them to accomplish in the world. With strategic awareness, an organization's strategic plan becomes a guidepost for carrying out the organization's vision while remaining flexible to changes in the organization and the world.

A powerful vision makes your organization, your products, and your service solution unique. It generates conditions that enable a constant flow of creativity instead of the churning out of yet another standardized product or service. Skeptics might say that the role of a powerful vision in business strategy development activities is nothing new. They would be correct. The importance of having a powerful vision is not a new idea. It is the heart and soul of every successful person and organization. All great success begins with an intense vision. A compelling vision inspires you when you are low, directs you when you are feeling lost, and provides guidance to the tasks at hand. A powerful vision induces you to take action to make the vision a reality, no matter what obstacles you encounter. Most important, your vision leads to the generation of new ideas that expand your business and improve the lives of your stakeholders, your clients, and the world. Those who fail to generate a powerful vision are destined to be eternal followers.

A culture of strategic awareness cannot exist without an inspiring and bold vision. How often do you hear people say, "Our vision guides all our strategic decision making" or "Our vision is what holds the organization together" or "The people in our organization really get our vision and work with us to achieve it"? Not very often, we'd guess. Yet isn't this what vision statements are for—to guide organizational decision making, hold an organization together, and assist people to achieve shared purposes or aspirations? A bold vision has a way of inspiring team members and stakeholders. It must be an expression of what your organization sees as a possibility and a future for the community and stakeholders you serve. Once a vision statement has been created, then all decisions and potential projects and services can be filtered through it to assess whether they are truly vision-driven and facilitate the possible future and impact your organization desires.

The key dynamics that will assure your business' success are the vision you have established and your employees' ability to align with that vision. In a successful organization, everyone is committed to the same vision and uses their energy to forward that common vision. Instead of people working against each other, everyone adds their capacities and contributions to everybody else's. The result: A company capable of great things.

The same can be said for your personal vision. Your personal vision starts with perceiving what you love to do and knowing what makes your heart sing. Your vision sets up the foundation for the way you create your business and your life. Sometimes your personal vision creates the organizational vision (especially if you are the founder or the CEO). When you have a clear vision, you feel a surge of energy and excitement. It's the same thrill you felt as a child before a fun day out or an exciting holiday. If something is not exciting, why would you want to set out on the journey in the first place? The beauty of having clear vision is that it frees you to accept a wider variety of projects and pursuits, because you can remain true to your vision regardless of the form your work takes. Steve Jobs acknowledges the value of vision and knowing what you really love to do at the commencement address that he made to Stanford's 2005 graduating class:

> *I was lucky. I found what I loved to do early in life.... You've got to find what you love, and that is as true for work as it is for your lovers. Your work is going to fill a large part of your life, and the only way to be truly satisfied is to do what you believe is great work, and the only way to do great work is to love what you do. If you haven't found it yet, keep looking, and don't settle. As with all matters of the heart, you'll know when you find it, and like any great relationship, it just gets better and better as the years roll on. So keep looking. Don't settle....*
>
> *When I was 17 I read a quote that went something like "If you live each day as if it was your last, someday you'll most certainly be right." It made an impression on me, and since then, for the past 33 years, I have looked in the mirror every morning and asked myself, "If today were the last day of my life, would I want to do what I am about to do today?" And whenever the answer has been "no" for too many days in a row, I know I need to change something. Remembering that I'll be dead soon is the most important thing I've ever encountered to help me make the big choices in life, because almost everything—all external expectations, all pride, all fear of embarrassment or failure—these things just fall away in the face of death, leaving only what is truly*

important. Remembering that you are going to die is the best way I know to avoid the trap of thinking you have something to lose. You are already naked. There is no reason not to follow your heart.

Here are some questions that will help you to develop a clear and powerful personal vision. Ask yourself these questions and see what comes out:

- *What do you love to do so much that you can't wait for the sun to rise to do it?*

- *What would you do even if you didn't get paid for doing it?*

- *What is so easy for you to do, that you think everyone can do it?*

- *What skills, abilities, and capacities do you have that you think have no value?*

- *What do you really, really want for yourself and your business?*

- *What did you want to be when you were a kid?*

- *If you knew you couldn't fail, what would you like to do in the next five years?*

- *What impact do you want your organization to have on the communities you serve?*

3. The Ability to Extrapolate

The ability to extrapolate is a key asset in a business world that is changing at the speed of light—and it's also an essential ingredient of strategic awareness. Extrapolation is the ability to use what is already known to capture the intangible. Successful extrapolators perceive beyond the obvious. They look at what is, and at the same time, they see far over the horizon. They see things others miss because they have a highly developed capacity for detecting patterns in the external environment. They are masterful at perceiving the elements of something and figuring out how they can use those elements to create a different possibility. They assimilate and integrate patently unrelated ideas from different fields and recognize developing trends before they seem directly relevant.

Extrapolation is not problem solving. It's the opposite of trying to figure things out. It's a way of being, in which you are always observing and questioning. You are voraciously curious, willing to receive everything and open to outcomes. Extrapolation also requires you to be vulnerable, which means you are willing to let go of being in control. Extrapolation comes from breaking through the mental barrier constructed by obvious solutions. To successfully extrapolate, you must be willing to go outside the common business practices. You adopt a stance of spontaneity and openness. You are willing to receive without resistance or preconception.

Thomas Edison was a great extrapolator—as well as one of the most prolific inventors in history. He was also a very successful businessman. He had to be, to turn his inventions into innovative long lasting, practical items. He knew that his invention of a long lasting light bulb alone wouldn't change the world since the existing gas lighting system had captured the real power. He became aware that to be successful he had to generate an electrical power system by providing, on demand, light and power to everyone. He constructed power stations to convert steam power to electricity as well as generated the entire infrastructure needed to support the use of electricity.

Edison did not actually invent the first light bulb as is sometimes said— but through the process of extrapolation, he developed the filaments that made long-lasting, practical electric light bulbs a reality. In what seems to us a wonderful example of extrapolation, the idea for using threads of carbonized bamboo as a raw material for the filaments occurred to him while he was relaxing on the shore of a lake and remembered the bamboo threads on the fishing pole he had used as a boy. We see a similar capacity to extrapolate in Steve Jobs, whose ability to successfully connect seemingly unrelated ideas from different fields enabled him to generate remarkable ideas.

Jeffrey H. Dyer, Hal B. Gregersen, and Clayton M. Christensen wrote in the Harvard Business Review (December 2009) that the number one skill that separates remarkable people from normal people is their ability to successfully connect seemingly unrelated questions, problems, or ideas from different fields.

They undertook a six-year study and interviewed 3,000 executives in an attempt to uncover the origins of creative—and often disruptive—business strategies in particularly innovative companies. Here is what they had to say:

> *When you ask creative people how they did something, they feel a little guilty because they didn't really do it; they just saw something. That's because they were able to connect experiences they've had. And the reason they were able to do that was that they've had more experiences or they had thought more about their experiences than other people. A lot of people in our industry haven't had very diverse experiences. So they don't have enough dots to connect, and they end up with very linear solutions without a broad perspective on the problem.*

Great extrapolators live in the question and ask unbounded questions. This is very different from defined or targeted questions related to business functions. Unbounded questions do not seek the right answers. Unbounded questions seek to go beyond what is currently known. Great extrapolators constantly ask questions that challenge common wisdom or, as Tata Group chairman Ratan Tata puts it, they "question the unquestionable." The question is the magical ingredient.

Extrapolators are different to configurators, who take new information and try to fit it into the model or configuration they currently have. They come to conclusions and judgments as a way being "right" and then stop receiving other possibilities. Remember: Whenever you make a decision, conclusion, or judgment, you won't allow anything that that doesn't match that decision, judgment, or conclusion to come into your awareness. Decision, conclusion, or judgment build walls that block you from seeing what is possible. Extrapolation transpires when you let go of the need to conclude and judge, when you lessen the need to get the right answer, truly experience what you are seeing, and open yourself to the unexpected. When you do not claim, own, and acknowledge your ability to extrapolate, you bankrupt your business of possibilities.

To be a successful leader in the current environment, you have to be open to the signs that your business is being shifted or needs to be. You must have a clear perspective about where the external landscape might be going. You have to perceive the nature of change and then either take advantage of this dynamic or adapt to it. You must be able to perceive new ways to think about the market, emerging technologies, and different ways of conducting your business. You have to be willing to receive a different possibility. Your ability to extrapolate is critical to conceiving these possibilities. Six attributes of great extrapolators:

1. They pursue new experiences. They make a conscious choice to travel into unexplored territory. They are willing to leave their comfort zone, physically and mentally.

2. They live in the question and ask unbounded questions. They do not seek the right answer.

3. They think differently about common, everyday problems.

4. They are voraciously curious.

5. They are willing to be vulnerable and ready to let go of the old notion of being in control.

6. They are masterful at connecting seemingly unrelated ideas from different fields. They are proficient at synthesizing new things.

4. The Desire to Be a Contribution

Don't start a business just because everybody else is doing it or [because] it looks like it's a way to make a lot of money. Start a business because you found something you really love doing and have a passion for. Start a business because you found something unique that you can do better than anyone else. And start a business because you really want to make a big contribution to society over a long period of time.
~ Michael Dell

Whenever leaders ask us to facilitate their team in developing a strategic plan, the first thing we ask is, "What is your organization's vision, and is it working for you?" Looking at an organization's vision immediately allows us to see whether they have chosen to be a contribution to the world at large—or whether they have chosen to be inward and focused on the organization itself. An organization's vision is intrinsically ideological and predisposed towards a clear aspiration of how the world should be. It strongly reflects the personal culture of the organization.

By and large, the vision of organizations that subscribe to the business-as-usual paradigm tend to be an expression of competition and scarcity that is based on the aspiration to be the best in their industry and number one in the marketplace. This business-as-usual idea of vision is about competing, staying alive, winning and losing, and surviving in a world of scarcity and limited possibility. A vision statement like this propels the organization into a state of constant motion to create the context in which they fit, benefit, win, and/or lose. It compels them to see competition as the vehicle to success and promotes the scarcity and survivalist mentality of contextual reality.

Another way to generate a vision statement is from prosperity consciousness and the desire to be a contribution. Being a contribution is actually the cornerstone of strategic awareness. The full benefits of leading with strategic awareness come only to leaders who approach every moment with a deep sense of generosity of spirit and the desire to be a contribution.

In our quest to generate change and transformation in the world as social change agents, we studied business leaders who have generated affirmative change in the world. Our research confirms that leaders who generate phenomenal success as well as transformational change tend to operate beyond competing. Instead of following a conventional business-as-usual approach, they strive to generate success and transformational change beyond the bottom line. Being a contribution is a generative and dynamic way of leading people and business that is guaranteed to transform you as well as your staff and your organization.

Most people think that being a contribution means doing something for others or sharing in the work. This is not the case. Being a contribution is a way of being. When you choose to live your life and conduct your business from the space of being a contribution, you are improving the quality of life generally. Are you willing to live from the consciousness of being contribution? When you choose to be a contribution, soon your being will change and begin to resonate with your new state of consciousness.

Being a contribution is the simultaneity of gifting and receiving. By this we mean that you contribute energy unlimitedly, which then allows you to receive unlimitedly. According to Gary Douglas, the founder of Access Consciousness, people have considered contribution as just receiving or as giving and taking. This is a misidentification and misapplication of what contribution is. The essential feature of being a contribution is that no exchange occurs. When we are being a contribution, we don't have any expectation that the other person will give us anything in return. Contribution is when it's a joy to do things. People who are contributing never care whether they get anything back. They just really enjoy the process of contributing. They contribute and in the process they receive simultaneously. We can see contribution in a mother nursing her baby, in disaster relief efforts, in a gardener joyfully watering the garden, and in a teacher caringly supporting the young student.

To truly be a contribution requires you to have a willingness to receive from everyone who is willing to contribute to you. You also have to be willing to contribute to people who are willing to receive without judgment. When you do this, you open up to receiving from everything in the universe, not just the person you have contributed to. Most importantly, if you contribute to your own life, you will be a contribution to others as well. Contribution is about a joyful expression of life, a sense of expansiveness, a joy of being, and a sense of abundance in all things. If you really are not happy in the work you are doing or if you are doing your current job just for money, you are not being a contribution to the business. When you engage in doing something you don't really want to do, it creates obligation, expectation, projection, judgment, separation, and rejection. Can you imagine what it would be like if your whole life was based on the joy of it and there was no other reason or justification?

Why is being contribution so powerful? When you become a contribution, you consistently generate strategies that unlock the creativity of a wide range of people within your organization and beyond. You open your awareness to different possibilities that allow you to contribute what will create awareness for you, for the planet, and everyone else. When you are being a contribution as a leader, you are in the question. Here are some questions you can ask:

- *What contribution can I be?*

- *What contribution can we be? What contribution can our organization be?*

- *What contribution can I be to another?*

- *What contribution can they be to my business?*

- *Is this a contribution to their life?*

- *How much consciousness can we create here?*

- *What is the future we would wish for our community?*

- *What lasting legacy do we desire for our community?*

- *What can I choose here that would be a contribution?*

- *What question can I ask that will facilitate my being a contribution?*

When leaders are being a contribution, they free their organization from the dogma of competition-based strategy and help it chart its future strategy with awareness. When your business is built upon being a contribution you, your team, and your stakeholders are more motivated to take action, seek beyond the obvious and concentrate on the big picture, not just the numbers.

Being a contribution in a business does not mean being the source of it. When leaders choose to be the source, everything begins and ends with them. They tend to do everything in the business and cling to familiar territory and stereotypical answers. They are the answer. It is dangerous for leaders to become the source because this can lead to micromanagement, where they attempt to control every department, task, event, activity, plan— the entire business. They focus on understanding how to make existing processes (the status quo) work a little better rather than asking what they can do differently. The organization that is directed by this type of leader can easily degenerate into bureaucracy.

Leaders who function from being a contribution recognize that there is no right way and no wrong way. There are just ways, just different points of view. No fixed position, no form, no structure, and no significance allow leaders to see life as an exciting adventure that they can explore enthusiastically and deeply. They do everything from the place of conscious contribution and generosity of spirit, which invites the whole world to function with them, not against them.

Never underestimate the power of being a contribution to move your business and society forward. You can be a contribution to your business and the world at large by recognizing what will create the greatest change and facilitating that.

How Can You Expand Your Strategic Awareness?

Now that we've talked about the four primary attributes that set strategically aware leaders apart from others, let's talk about more specific ways you can develop and expand your strategic awareness. There are six simple practices that lead to the expansion of strategic awareness. They require no great amount of brainpower, no particular level of education, and little exertion or effort.

Constantly expose yourself to new experiences. *Place yourself in unfamiliar surroundings or in the midst of unusual or exotic experiences. Let go of your habitual mental routines. Learn to think differently about everyday things. Practice looking at common situations and common problems in novel ways.*

Be willing to be vulnerable. *Remain open to the new, the unfamiliar, and the unknown all around you. Be open to all possibility. Be willing to look at what you can do that will generate different possibilities.*

Cultivate a sense of curiosity, awe, wonderment, and amazement. *Embrace change. Be willing to step outside your comfort zone and preconceptions. Strategic awareness is the ability to relate to life in spontaneous interaction with the energy of the moment and have the ability to perceive, know, be, and receive everything.*

Be flexible and spontaneous. *Choose to be ever aware and mindful, ready to shift strategy and tactics as the situation requires.*

Question everything. *Ask "what if" questions such as "If I chose this, what would ensue?" Ask questions that challenge conventional norms and standard practices. Look beyond your best practices or your current market segments. Go beyond your existing customers to those who face constraints that inhibit their ability to solve the problems they* *face. As Peter Drucker said, "The customer rarely buys what the business thinks it sells him." Look for a job to be done or an important problem that is not adequately solved by current solutions.*

Live in the question. *Ask questions like "What do I need to be aware of here? Where is everyone functioning from? What contribution can I be? What is going to be generative for my business and for me in my life?" Questions will allow you to have awareness of the big picture and explicit insight into the situation at hand.*

Bring awareness into reality. *You can open and expand your strategic awareness by learning to listen and act upon it.*

Reflection

Strategic awareness requires transcending the cognitive mind, points of view, thoughts, feelings, and emotions. When leaders choose to live in the question, they start to become aware of potential choices and possibilities in the marketplace that were previously imperceptible and hidden. Here are a few questions that will assist you to begin your process of generating your strategic plan with strategic awareness.

Does your organization have an explicit and inspiring business vision that your stakeholders and team members enthusiastically embrace and support? What kind of effect will this vision have on the business and on the community? What effect will it have on your industry? What effect will it have on the company position, market value and share price?

What is your personal vision? Is your vision about making a positive impact on people's lives and leaving the world a better place than you found it? What contribution can you be? What do you perceive is possible for you to accomplish in the world? How will this personal vision impact your community, stakeholders, and society generally?

What is it possible for you to generate here? What products or services will there be? This question is about what's possible as opposed to what's likely. This is not about goal setting. In our view goal setting is about establishing fixed points of view that tend to be limited by your experience.

What's not working? What do we need to do about it? What needs to change? Is there anything in our business that we have always wanted to generate or change that we have never been able to achieve?

What are the opportunities that are already apparent in the local market, in the industry, in the society, and in the global market? What if everything was the opposite of what it appeared to be?

What resources do we require and where are they? Do they have to be our resources? What if the resources required were totally different from what we have already decided they should be?

What will be our indicators of success?

What additional questions should we be asking? What have we missed?

CHAPTER TWELVE

Beyond The Bottom line

Of the billionaires I have known, money just brings out the basic traits in them. If they were jerks before they had money, they are simply jerks with a billion dollars.
~ Warren Buffett

Earlier in our careers, in our quest to become social change agents who contributed to the world, we focused our energy on being a contribution and doing good deeds with little or no attention on attaining personal wealth. Although we didn't realize it at the time, we were ensnared in this contextual reality. We had bought the viewpoint that attaining wealth and being a contribution were mutually exclusive. In other words, we had allowed ourselves to be defined by the circumstances of the world around us. We didn't want to be known as capitalists because in the current environment, capitalism was widely perceived as greedy, selfish, exploitative, uncaring, and interested only in maximizing profits. We had been sticking ourselves with the points of view we had bought from others that it was more virtuous and honorable to give than to receive. We had somehow bought the point of view that we needed to create our business from being benevolent and that it is not decent to make a lot of money at the same time. Over the years we have been able to disentangle ourselves from this bizarre perspective. We became aware that a balance was needed between benevolence and capitalism. Business today needs a new paradigm along the lines of benevolent capitalism, because it is apparent that conventional business practices are out of balance—and we need to address this imbalance now. Business as usual is not working anymore.

Although it may seem that the only way to secure one's financial future is to buy into contextual reality and pursue the business-as-usual paradigm, the paradox is that if business leaders remain locked within the current business-as-usual model, they risk their survival by creating an anti-conscious future. Benevolent capitalism will distinguish the vanguard from the old guard. Capitalism must morph into being more responsible, transparent, and benevolent. It must embody greater generosity of spirit. Organizations must be governed more consciously and with a greater social and environmental responsibility as they attempt to secure financial prosperity.

What Is Benevolent Capitalism?

So, what exactly is benevolent capitalism? And how is it different from traditional capitalism? First we need to look at the concept and meaning of capitalism and whether capitalism is good or bad. This seems to be a common debate, occurring in the general population throughout the world. According to *The American Heritage New Dictionary of Cultural Literacy,* capitalism is an economic system characterized by a free market for goods and services and private control of production and consumption. It is a system based on the principles of property rights, rule of law, voluntary exchange, wealth creation, and entrepreneurial initiative, and the human activity and social organizations (called businesses) reflecting and embodying these principles. From this definition, it is clear that capitalism, in and of itself, is value neutral. It is neither good nor bad. Capitalism can be the source for good when it is based on benevolence or it can be irresponsible and destructive if it is based on greed and the viewpoint that resources are scarce.

Benevolent capitalism is the emerging integration between awareness, prosperity consciousness, being a contribution, and capitalism. Benevolent capitalism sees business as a form of humanistic social organization: people getting together for an intent and objective, to do something together to create a generative world, by taking action based upon what we know— business and generosity of spirit.

Benevolent capitalism presents enormous opportunities, especially for business. It creates sustainable economies, a sustainable future for people and the planet, creates a greater change in the world, as well as improving business performance. Benevolent capitalism, in our view, is a form of capitalism that is driven by businesses which not only think about the short-term financial benefits but also about building longer-term sustainable businesses that create economic, environmental. and social value, that have a positive impact on society. This means ensuring that generosity of spirit and a conscious way of doing business are at the heart of all aspects of business operations. It must be ingrained into business strategy and practices.

Corporations can be described as practicing benevolent capitalism when they:

- *Have a commitment to society, community, and people*

- *Take care of their employees*

- *Possess a sincere and genuine aspiration for environmental preservation*

- *Contribute to sustainability for future generations*

- *Initiate economic transparency through the supply chain*

- *Provide quality-of-living products and services*

- *Deliver excellence in value to customers and stakeholders*

- *Enrich investors*

Organizations that embrace benevolent capitalism are conscious of how their actions impact their constituencies. Sure, they worry about their investors and shareholders, but they're also concerned about stakeholders like employees, customers, suppliers, and communities at home and abroad—as well as planet Earth.

When benevolence guides business principles, vision, and practices, the result can be exceedingly affirmative. Benevolent capitalism can be the very thing that helps to steer the planet away from suffering and towards a common flourishing. Corporations large and small, private and public, have an enormous power to shape this planet in a positive way. They can become the most powerful agents of change in the world when they embrace benevolent capitalism as a way of being.

Corporations also have potential to do immense harm to communities and the environment when their leaders operate from anti-consciousness or unconsciousness, which includes greed and short sightedness. It is the anti-consciousness of individual leaders that cause the damage and destruction—not the notion of capitalism itself. Business as usual at its base level is a competition, a struggle for energy and resources. It is done from the economics of scarcity. This way of operating has become conventional practice for most organizations generation upon generation.

There are many corporate executives and free market economists who maintain the view that the only social responsibility a law-abiding business has is to maximize profits for its shareholders. Many business leaders truly believe that maximizing profits for investors is the only acceptable justification for corporate actions. This impels them to focus on achieving short-term financial gain at almost any cost. They have not realized that a short-term, profit-only approach has its downsides, for the reason that greed tends to incur excessive exposure to hazards and doesn't maximize long-term results. This traditional approach to capitalism has accelerated the quantity and intensity of social and environmental problems that risk society's stability.

There is now a growing consensus that capitalism is out of balance, particularly in corporations that focus solely on financial gain to maximize shareholder value. While measuring profit and financial result is seen as fundamental, there are also deeper societal and environmental impact costs and returns to factor in. Sadly, the current commonly accepted business performance measurement systems are often not designed to take these into consideration. Executives who conduct business-as-usual fail to look beyond the scope of their immediate financial results. This traditional approach to capitalism is not sustainable.

An alternative business model is required, one that takes into consideration the value of an organization and its products to the wider community as well as its ability to be a contribution to consciousness. In Charles Dickens' famous novel, *The Christmas Carol*, Ebenezer Scrooge, the miserly, mean-spirited main character, is visited one Christmas Eve by three ghosts who attempt to show him the error of his ways. The first ghost is his deceased business partner, Jacob Marley. Marley's ghost is full of regret and recrimination about the way he lived. Scrooge attempts to reassure him and says, "But you were always a good man of business, Jacob." Jacob replies:

> *Business! Mankind was my business. The common welfare was my business; charity, mercy, forbearance, and benevolence were all my business. The dealings of my trade were but a drop of water in the comprehensive ocean of my business.*

Like Marley, business leaders must recognize that an important part of their success is connected to the power and affirmative impact that they have on their communities. Leaders in charge of organizations must become more aware of the consequences of the financial doctrine that emphasizes the desirability of short-term gains. They must work towards more than just financial reward. At the root of all needed change lays the level of consciousness of those making the decisions. A corporation reflects the awareness and mirrors the consciousness of its leaders and executives. Benevolent capitalism requires a comprehensive and thorough transformation in consciousness on the part of the corporate executives engaged in any business venture. As leaders and executives grow in prosperity consciousness, so do the organizations they lead. Unless business leaders willingly change their consciousness, business-as-usual will continue.

While we may deplore anti-conscious business practices, they still constitute the standard business model for many commercial and public sector organizations around the world. Many of these organizations still operate from on the old "How do I fit? How do I benefit? How do I win? and How do I lose?" paradigm. They often seek to retain all the benefits of doing business while refusing to see the injury and the damage they have done. Settling for the conventional business practices in order to maintain the status quo seems to be the prevalent state of mind of many conventional business executives today.

The reality is, most organizations are still devotees of the old business-as-usual paradigm. They uphold the belief that time-honored capitalists earn the highest return on investment. They are captives of a business model that values financial gain more than anything else. They tend to carry out policies that emphasize the advantage gained by short-term profit. They are content with pulling off the company's profit objectives and tend to ignore the social cost of achieving them.

The avalanche of corporate scandals that have rocked the markets recently has illustrated that worldly power without consciousness, goodwill, benevolence, and generosity of spirit are the downfall of capitalism. Sadly, these scandals have helped to perpetuate the image of capitalism as greedy, selfish, exploitative, uncaring—and interested only in maximizing profits. Because of this perception, many people have come to the conclusion that the purpose of business is solely to maximize profits for the investors. They believe corporations only want to dominate and control the world. For those who adopt this line of thinking, it follows that corporate power is a highly destructive force in society, since corporations are greedy, selfish, and uncaring. Capitalism is therefore not a positive force in the world. But what if this doesn't have to be the case? What if there is much more to capitalism than conventional business people knew—or even cared to know—is possible?

The Radical Imperative

Benevolent capitalism sounds lofty. Is it practical? Our response is a resounding, yes! It is truly practical and highly attainable. Truth is, many corporations have already implemented an all-encompassing, corporation-wide philosophy of benevolent capitalism. Standout examples include Starbucks, Whole Foods Market, Aveda, Gaiam, and Nordstrom. These organizations recognize that their success is linked to the powerful and positive impact that they have on the communities and the world. They work consciously to ensure that their vision and values guide their day-to-day business decisions.

Starbucks and Whole Foods Market are the top players in the transformation of capitalism. They symbolize the principles of benevolent capitalism that many corporations can emulate and they repeatedly earn a strong spot on Fortune's "100 Best Companies to Work For" list. Both Starbucks and Whole Foods Market believe that businesses can—and should—have a positive impact on the communities they serve as well as the world at large. They fulfill their visions by:

- *Supporting and investing in local neighborhoods and global communities through strategic partnerships and economic development opportunities that deepen their ties in the communities where they do business.*

- *Committing to minimize their environmental impact, tackle climate change, and inspire others to do the same.*

- *Creating a workplace that values and respects people from diverse backgrounds and enabling their employees to do their best work.*

- *Honoring the unique combination of the talents, experience, and perspective of each employee, making business success possible.*

Neither Starbucks nor Whole Foods Market claim perfection, but both are continuously evaluating and refining their relationships with customers, suppliers, employees, and the environment across a broad spectrum. They endeavor to get their actions more in line with a vision of providing for the greatest good for all.

In the case of Starbucks, making a positive environmental and social contribution has been a vision and guiding principle of the company since it was founded more than thirty years ago. It has endorsed the principles of benevolent capitalism by taking a strong stand on social and environmental issues and by holding itself publicly accountable for delivering on its commitment. Starbucks has demonstrated that there is no conflict between financial success and generosity of spirit.

Whole Foods Market represents another compelling example of ways corporations can thrive financially while contributing consciously and positively to the environment, communities, and the world. John Mackey, the founder and CEO of Whole Foods Market, sees no incongruity between benevolence and profitability. In fact, he sees profits as a means to the end for giving life to Whole Foods' social aspiration. Mackey wrote in a blog in September 2005:

> *Making high profits is the means to the end of fulfilling Whole Foods' core business mission. We want to improve the health and well being of everyone on the planet through higher-quality foods and better nutrition, and we can't fulfill this mission unless we are highly profitable. High profits are necessary to fuel our growth across the United States and the world. Just as people cannot live without eating, so a business cannot live without profits. But most people don't live to eat, and neither must a business live just to make profits. . . . Whole Foods Market was not created solely to maximize profits for its investors, but to create value for all of its stakeholders. I believe there are thousands of other businesses similar to Whole Foods (Medtronic, REI, and Starbucks, for example) that were created by entrepreneurs with goals beyond maximizing profits, and that these goals are neither "hypocritical" nor "cloaking devices" but are intrinsic to the purpose of the business.*

The fastest growing supermarket in the world, Whole Foods Market's business model explicitly calls for serving not just shareholders, but customers, employees, vendors/suppliers, the community, and the environment. This allegiance to a benevolent way of being has helped Whole Food Market produce impressive benefits for the organization and for the broader social world. Whole Foods' business vision is based on the seemingly contrarian principles of transparency, community, and social equality, autonomy, appreciation, caring, egalitarianism, and respect.

The beauty of benevolent capitalism is that generosity of spirit and profitability cannot only coexist; they can thrive simultaneously. Starbucks and Whole Foods Market have repeatedly achieved financial returns that beat the market and their rivals, proving that benevolence and capitalism may be peculiarly companionable after all. Benevolence and capitalism are not mutually exclusive. These companies and others like them provide little doubt that benevolent capitalism is simply good business and works for the long-term benefit of investors.

The Foundations of Benevolence

To embrace the principle of benevolent capitalism, we must first of all acknowledge that the notion that capitalism, in itself, is value neutral. It is undeniable that money and capitalism make the world work. Modern society works because capitalism exists. Most people today would agree that, on balance, capitalism has provided tremendous benefits and great progress to our communities and the world. It creates an environment in which societal welfare is enhanced and individuals can achieve and excel. However, the ongoing financial crisis since 2008 has uncovered fundamental flaws in the traditional capitalist system. Business leaders need to wake up to the fact that the capitalist system and industrial growth as we have known it, is now encountering severe social and environmental limits. Businesses have a choice to make. They can keep focusing on the short term narrow objective of maximizing profits. Or, they can choose to become a benevolent capitalist. To ensure viable and sustainable businesses in a more generative economy, leaders are required to choose to increase the speed and scale of change towards benevolent capitalism and operate in a more conscious way. This means ensuring that the benevolent capitalism way of doing business is at the heart of all aspects of business operations and business strategy, and not just because it is politically correct.

Research conducted by Edelman's annual global survey of consumers (a point of view on the evolving relationship between business, brands, and society to create mutual social responsibility and sustainable value) clearly indicates that consumers worldwide increasingly expect companies to invest in social good, to serve the community in ways beyond the products and services they provide.

> *86 percent of global consumers believe that business needs to place at least equal weight on society's interests as on business' interests. 64 percent believe it is no longer enough for corporations to give money; they must integrate good causes into their everyday business.*
> *~2010 Edelman goodpurpose© Study*

We now have the opportunity to create a new capitalism that will do what people and the world need capitalism to do:

> *to create a generative economic system that will create meaningful jobs for all those who want them;*

> *to consciously manage social, environmental, and economic impacts in their supply chain;*

> *to consistently taking action to reduce climate change;*

> *and to provide products and services with improved social and environmental impacts, as well as positively influencing people's life.*

These are the opportunities. Today's companies that are led by conscious and benevolent leaders understand this. From Grameen Bank to Starbucks, from Nordstrom to Whole Foods, from Proctor & Gamble (P&G) to the Container Store, from Apple to Google, these companies are generating every form of value that matters—emotional, social, and financial. And they're doing it for all stakeholders. Not because it's "politically correct," but because it's the ultimate path to long-term strategic advantage. Benevolent capitalists are conscious of how their actions impact their constituencies, their communities, and the world at large. Sure, they care about shareholders, and they also care about "stakeholders" that include employees, customers, suppliers, communities at home and abroad—and planet Earth.

To embrace the principle of benevolent capitalism, we must first of all acknowledge that the notion that capitalism, in itself, is value neutral. It is neither inherently good nor bad. It is simply an economic system in which investment and ownership of the means of production, distribution, and exchange of wealth is made and maintained by private individuals or corporations. Capitalism can be a force for good when it is based on benevolence and prosperity consciousness—or it can be extremely irresponsible and destructive if it is based on greed and a scarcity viewpoint.

We believe that in order to embrace the principle of benevolent capitalism, which we see as source of great benefit on the planet, we must refrain from demonizing capitalism. A sincere gratitude and appreciation for what it can bring to the world is therefore a great place to start.

Everything Is Connected

Benevolent capitalism can become the leading edge of business transformation. Leaders who operate with strategic awareness and prosperity consciousness can lead the way to a more life-affirming way of doing business that supports a "triple bottom line" of people, planet, and profit, where the focus is on in creating value for customers, employees, communities, and the planet as well as shareholders and partners.

In other words, they can help to develop capitalism that works for the common good in addition to making a profit. To do this, they must focus on the value they generate for all eight of their most important stakeholders:

1. *Clients*

2. *Team members (employees)*

3. *Investors*

4. *Suppliers*

5. *Communities*

6. *Humanity*

7. *The environment*

8. *The planet*

In an increasingly complex and dynamic global market, prosperity consciousness is needed more than ever. It is the consciousness of corporate leaders that must be addressed and changed, as consciousness is senior to matter. The world is changing rapidly and each business will undergo hardship or experience abundant success depending upon its leader's consciousness and actions. Leaders' consciousness determines their circumstances, their surroundings, and their state of affairs. Unless leaders' consciousness changes, everything will remain the same.

As we mentioned in Chapter Four, a basic truth of the universe, confirmed by discoveries in quantum physics, is that we are connected to each and every being and to each molecule upon this planet, and every one of them supports us and the energy and power that we are. Everything is connected. Things exist through their relationships with one another. Every component in this universe has the potential to affect all the other components. We cannot move without influencing everything in our universe. We cannot even observe anything without changing the object and ourselves. Quantum physicists discovered that the simple process of observation is sufficient to cause infinitesimal particles at the subatomic level to alter and transform. In this interconnected universe, establishing and enhancing our prosperity consciousness means that a shift in our conscious awareness can simultaneously reverberate into the widest global environment to subtly engage and transform everyone.

The butterfly effect, which was discovered in chaos theory, (a field of mathematics) has shown ways in which a minute change in one place can result in large differences to a later state. For example, as farfetched as it may seem, a butterfly flapping its wings in Australia could lead to creation or absence of a hurricane in America. If a single butterfly can set in motion such an astonishing consequence on the Earth, consider how large an effect you and your business could have on the world at large. You can have an effect not only by choosing conscious actions, but also by using your power to be the change agent you truly are.

The current financial collapses and global environmental dilemmas have been driven by anti-consciousness and human negligence. Prosperity consciousness can break new ground here, bringing awareness, generosity of spirit, stewardship, and a sense of benevolence to bear on the flows of business ventures, products, and services. Organizations that function from prosperity consciousness and think globally are positioning themselves for immediate and sustainable growth.

If you are to evolve beyond the limitations put in place by contextual reality, you have to break out of the boundaries that define how you should create your business. Accelerating short-term profit in a vacuum or working exclusively to grow revenue is no longer acceptable. The world requires a different, all-inclusive vision and practice that will contribute to society's advancement and well being. Business leaders must find a way to step beyond contextual reality and the bottom line. The business principles you choose to embrace can represent a more benevolent form of capitalism, one that reliably works for the common good.

Be a Generative Element in the World

Energy, space, and consciousness are the source for generation of new possibilities. Generation is continuous energy and continuous expansion of possibilities, which is what consciousness is, which is what pure energy is, which is what space is. Generation is like being a battery, an electrical current, a never-ending supply of energy that is constantly flowing.
~ Gary Douglas

Nordstrom is an amazing demonstration of a corporation that has achieved phenomenal success and is also making a positive contribution to society and the world. They have created space for greater possibilities by establishing clear leadership, governance, and values and integrating conscious and benevolent business practices across all of their business operations. They have created a number of programs and initiatives that are currently in place or part of their future plans. This is a very different paradigm for creating and generating a totally different reality.

Nordstrom has embraced the benevolent capitalism way of being by focusing on four key "pillars" as described on their website:

1. Supporting Communities – *They have been investing in the communities in which their business operates and those communities in greatest need. They have been working with United Way for nearly 60 years to help make a difference in communities. They have also formed partnerships with industry organizations, service providers, and other retailers to help make a positive, sustainable impact through a variety of innovative programs.*

2. Sustaining the Environment – *They have developed strategy to conserve natural resources by focusing on reducing greenhouse gases and using energy, water, and forest resources efficiently. They've been recycling corrugated cardboard, office paper, mixed paper, metals, lamps, and pallets/wood in their distribution and fulfillment centers since 1999.*

3. Protecting Human Rights – *They collaborate with many partners (factories, subcontractors, employees, and other manufacturer/retailers) to help ensure that their core business standards and all applicable laws regarding health, safety, and fair workplaces are upheld. They created the Nordstrom Social Responsibility team in 1994. This team works closely with the Nordstrom Product Group (NPG) manufacturers and vendors to ensure that Nordstrom-label products are made in accordance with all applicable laws and ethical labor practices.*

4. Caring for their People – *They began a profit-sharing program with employees from 1952. They have established efforts with industry peers to consistently improve working conditions in the factories and communities where they source Nordstrom products.*

Nordstrom is preparing to open an innovative new department store in downtown Manhattan that will donate all of its profits to charity. This example is important because the company is not only able to contribute to good works in the world, it also is able to apply its brand power and deeply intuitive knowledge of retail and the American consumer to create an experience around shopping to do good. Nordstrom is setting a precedent for other mainstream corporations in applying their business expertise to doing their part to contribute to a better and more sustainable world community.

Prosperity Consciousness as a State of Being

Phenomenal successes all begin with prosperity consciousness—and it's just as important for individuals as it is for corporations. In our work with individuals of diverse backgrounds and businesses of all sizes and types, we have discovered that the primary difference between remarkably prosperous people and the rest of the crowd is the choices they make. Prosperous people have chosen to perceive, know, be, and receive themselves as the contributor and generator of their life. They have claimed, owned, and acknowledged that they are responsible for their situation and the things they create. They never blame external circumstances, their past, or their background for what they are.

Prosperous and successful leaders know that there is an abundance of money and a never-ending array of business opportunities. There is more than enough for all—an endless supply. Benevolent capitalists like Steve Jobs, Richard Branson, and Warren Buffett have prosperity consciousness. They don't buy into the lie of scarcity or erroneous beliefs about insufficiency that are based on the appearance of poverty in this reality. If they had believed the lie of scarcity, they would never have even thought it was possible for them to become phenomenally successful. The belief in scarcity tends to shrink the perception of opportunities, whereas the belief in prosperity expands it extensively.

What would make a company a benevolent capitalist enterprise? Excellent wages, excellent benefits, adequate vacation time, tuition re-reimbursement, a social conscience about their products and procedures, a desire to better their communities, a reasonable compensation for the upper tier of executives, and a return on investment for shareholders to let them know they can support a benevolent company and still make money doing it.

Prosperity consciousness is not an extraordinary privilege that is bestowed to some people and not to others. It is an attainable state of being that is available to everyone—if they choose to claim, own, and acknowledge it. Virtually anyone can develop and expand their prosperity consciousness if they choose. If you want your organization to operate with strategic awareness and prosperity consciousness, then you must walk the talk. You must choose to lead from this space. All the prosperous and successful people we know confirm that taking responsibility for being the creator of their own reality is the key to having a prosperous and successful life.

We have discovered over decades of working in this area, that more than anything else, people are held back from being prosperous and successful by their viewpoints about money, prosperity, and abundance. It is not because they were born into a poor family or because they didn't get a college education or because they were disadvantaged to begin with. This does not mean that we have to work to amass an immense fortune, but we all can if we so choose. A person with an expanded prosperity consciousness may choose to live simply, free of trauma or distress, apprehension or money concerns. The choice is ours. Those who have developed a prosperity consciousness simply choose that which will be a contribution to their life and to the world at large.

A State of Your Being

The foundation of benevolent capitalists' accomplishment is their prosperity consciousness. They have claimed, owned, and acknowledged prosperity consciousness as a state of their being. They trust something that most others don't—their awareness. They also trust that the appropriate people, prospects, and possibilities will come their way. They know that money is easy to attract. There is an abundance of money and resources¾a never-ending supply. They take pleasure in having money. They enjoy the way they acquire money, receive money, use money, give money, and relate to money. They are a living magnet, and they invariably attract into their lives people, ideas, opportunities, and circumstances that are in harmony with their state of "beingness".

From a business venture and an investment perspective, you can know everything about business, investment, financial strategies, real estate, and the top secrets of high finance. However, if your awareness, or consciousness, concerning money is based on the scarcity paradigm, you will never have the sense that you have enough money. Moreover, if somehow you are able to acquire a lot of money, you most likely will not appreciate it, and in all probability, will not be able to retain it.

The good news is that you can choose to cultivate and expand your consciousness to create success and abundance. Everyone has the gift of free will and the freedom of choice. If you choose to be prosperous, you must believe and know that you are, and you must perceive and receive that you are, and soon the conditions of your reality will change to entrain with your consciousness.

I always knew I was going to be rich. I don't think I ever doubted it for a minute.
~ Warren Buffet

The lack of prosperity in many people's lives is due to the way they view money and resources. Their viewpoints about money, which are based in contextual reality, impose severe limitations on the prosperity they can experience. Contextual reality creates a world of judgments and beliefs that lead to a scarcity frame of mind. With the points of view they have adopted, they create for themselves a scarcity paradigm. Scarcity becomes a way of life for them, and they often experience a feeling of lack as part of their reality. And they bring this into their business and organization!

Prosperity conscious leaders stand apart in their willingness to engage in the task of continuously regenerating and rejuvenating their business. They do so with an expanded awareness for generating advancement in innovation, bottom-line profits, as well as social responsibility, and environmental stewardship—a combination that produces the most powerful generative edge and strategic advantage.

A Scarcity Mindset Leads to Competitive Thinking

A scarcity mindset is the cause of most kinds of misfortune. People who don't have prosperity consciousness have a chronic sense of insufficiency about life. This is the fundamental mode from which they think, act, and function in the world. They believe that in order to get what they want, they have to take it away from someone else. They also think that if they choose to do one thing, then they'll have to give up something else. They feel resentful when someone else has something they would like to have. They believe that if someone else has something they desire, then they themselves will have to go without. This scarcity point of view encourages competition, animosity, antagonism, and hostility. Believing that others' good fortune is a threat to theirs, they often try to rain on other people's parade or strive to bring others down. They are not aware that there is more than enough for everyone.

A scarcity mindset keeps people from perceiving and experiencing the ongoing natural state of abundance. It's the point of view that lack is more real than abundance. It may seem real—but it is not a reflection of how things really are. It's a state of mind we create. A scarcity mindset is not a state of mind that only "poor" people have. Rich people can have it as well. Surprisingly, many who are financially well off have a scarcity mindset, and no matter how much they have they are still afraid, untrusting, greedy, and stressed. In their mind there is never enough.

True prosperity consciousness brings with it a peaceful mind, a deep awareness, and an abiding trust that there will always be enough. Prosperity has its roots in benevolence, and scarcity has its roots in avarice. People who have a scarcity frame of mind have attitudes, mindsets, feelings, and values associated with lack or the fear of lack. They believe there is not enough to go around for everyone in the world. It is not easy for people to perceive different possibilities when they are convinced that there is not enough to go around¾especially when their points of view keep creating situations where they get to be right about how difficult life is! They assume that their reality of lack and scarcity is true, but nothing could be further from the actual truth.

Unlike prosperous people, those who function in the scarcity paradigm do not exercise their power of choice as a way of life. In fact, most people who have a scarcity mindset are not aware that they have choices at all. They don't know that they can choose the quality of their lives. The scope of what they can attain is limited by their lack of awareness and by what they fail to choose. Because they are not aware of what they don't know, there is little they can do to change. To them, change is unimaginable!

Reflection

Unless you are willing to make the shift from a scarcity mindset to prosperity consciousness, it is going to be business-as-usual, regardless of how much money you have. Until your consciousness concerning money changes, no matter how much money you create, your experience will remain the same.

A powerful way to begin to change your life and become prosperous is to start noticing what you expect to experience in life. Be aware of the consciousness you have about money. If you are honest with yourself, you will perceive and know whether or not your relationship with money is expansive and conscious.

To choose prosperity consciousness, pay no heed to what you find objectionable about your financial situation. Instead, focus on the unlimited, alternative possibilities and what you would like to generate. When you do this, you will begin to perceive and receive many new opportunities—and you will be able to act on them regardless of your reality concerning your financial situation has been up to that point.

So, what is it going to take for you to make a choice to be greater than your present situation?

What's it going to take for you to expand your prosperity consciousness?

CHAPTER THIRTEEN

All Things are Possible

Always you have been told that work is a curse and labor a misfortune. But I say to you that when you work you fulfill a part of earth's furthest dream, assigned to you when that dream was born. And in keeping yourself with labor you are in truth loving life. And to love life through labor is to be intimate with life's inmost secret.
~ Kahlil Gibran, twentieth-century Syrian-born mystic poet and philosopher

To embrace a no-more-business-as-usual paradigm and a benevolent capitalism way of being takes choice, boldness, strategic awareness, prosperity consciousness, the courage to stand-alone when the winds of popular opinion are against you, and the faith to believe in your vision in the face of overwhelming odds. The choice to change is not one of obligation but one of knowing that you have the power to change the construct of your business in light of this different vision of benevolent capitalism. It's awareness that to achieve thriving and generative success, you must reinvent the way business is conducted.

The saying, "All things are possible" is a remarkable and truthful maxim, but it isn't valuable unless you apply it to your life. The truth is; all things are possible only to the people who truly believe that is true. Your point of view shapes your life. It creates your reality. It creates your business the way it is. Your point of view about yourself and the way you react to your thoughts, feelings, and emotions throughout the day ground you in contextual reality—or open the door to the infinite possibilities that are available to you. For your business to change from the current business-as-usual paradigm to a no-more-business-as-usual paradigm, your leadership team must embrace a benevolent capitalism way of being. Leaders have to start thinking and acting differently. They have to be willing to embody the viewpoint and priority that profit and prosperity go hand in hand with community engagement, stakeholder orientation, social responsibility, and environmental stewardship. Your leadership team must stop focusing purely on the short term narrow objective of maximizing profits. They must be willing to be a contribution and acknowledge that their active participation in the creation of a generative future is the only thing that will allow the business to thrive and remain viable into the future.

Every business has the potential to embody the benevolent capitalism way of being. Business leaders can achieve this by choosing to create a more generative and expansive priority for their organization, which goes beyond bottom-line profits, convenience, or shareholder value. The most generative and prosperous businesses over the long-term consciously create value for all of their interdependent stakeholders—customers, employees, investors, suppliers, community, and the environment. Paradoxically, the benevolent capitalism way of being also creates the most long-term and generative value for investors. In the study presented in the book *Firms of Endearment: How World Class Companies Profit from Passion and Purpose*, (Sisodia, Wolfe & Sheth 2007), the authors discovered that such businesses outperformed the overall stock market by a 9 to 1 ratio over a ten-year period.

Everything we do can be done consciously, unconsciously, or anti-consciously. Capitalism and business ventures therefore can be practiced consciously, unconsciously, or anti-consciously. When the business is operated unconsciously or anti-consciously, it becomes exploitation, mishandling, abusive, and even fraud or deception. They tend to demonstrate a precarious lack of awareness, shortsightedness of vision, and superficiality of priority. Conversely, when the business is operated consciously, it can be an architect or a catalyst for making the world a better place as well as contribute to the greater good.

Before you can let go of business-as-usual, you must challenge anything that is not working in your business and your reality. Until now, you may have been unaware of the impact contextual reality was having on your point of view—and your business. Look as clearly and honestly as you can at the paradigm you and your teams predominantly utilize to view your business and the world around you. When you change your focus from business-as-usual to the benevolent capitalist paradigm, you can change your business situation, sometimes instantaneously.

The questions you should ask yourself before endeavoring to embody the benevolent capitalism way of being are:

> *Does your management team still believe that business is about competing, staying alive, winning, losing, and surviving in a world of scarcity and limited possibility? Is it possible that they have a fixed point of view based on past success that prevents them from seeing new and different possibilities?*

> *Does your leadership and management team operate based on contextual reality and accept as true the idea that other businesses in your chosen industry are your competitors and that you have to beat those competitors to succeed?*

> *Does your organization still maintain conventional strategies because you and your team believe your industry's structural characteristics are inflexible and your business boundaries are defined?*

The above questions are for facilitating awareness, to know the condition of your existing business. When you spend time sincerely looking at your business with these questions, you will start to have awareness of places where you can generate different possibilities. It is essential to never judge your business or your team for the way your business has been operating up until now, and do not defend or justify your existing situation, otherwise you will never be able to let it go and move on. If you acknowledge what is, then you can have other choices. You have all choices available when you acknowledge what you are doing and being, without judgment. If you do not judge, discriminate, or discern about anything, you are free to choose without a fixed point of view.

You have to get to interesting point of view about everything you have judged as wrong. If you look at your current business and the choices you have made so far and you go, "I didn't do that right", you have just gone to the judgment, made yourself wrong and made it right that you chose wrong. The judgment that you have made a wrong choice will stick you into contextual reality and into looking at what you did that you shouldn't have done, rather than "What do I wish to choose today?" What if you never judged what you did? What difference does it make if it was right or wrong? That was then and this is now. It's just what you chose. What would you like to choose now? When you recognize that "this isn't working", it requires you to ask "What can I do differently?" not "How do I fix it?" What you can do differently is in the non-contextual reality.

Leading the Change Process

To effectively activate the no-more-business-as-usual paradigm for your organization, there are certain priorities that you have to embrace. One priority is to acknowledge that your business has the potential for a higher purpose than just maximizing profits. If you are leading a change process, first and foremost you have to choose to embody and be a conscious leader both in your personal life and in your business. As mentioned earlier, you are going to need to change your point of view. You must be willing to see that your business has the potential for a more expansive vision and a more generative priority. Most importantly, you must be willing to acknowledge that the key priority of your business isn't just about maximizing profits or shareholder returns. You must be willing to lead and manage your business for the benefit of all of your interdependent stakeholders—customers, employees, investors, suppliers, community, the environment, and the world at large, not just shareholders. You must consider the impact your choices and business strategies will have on all the stakeholders. It takes conscious leadership, choice, awareness, ingenuity, and perseverance to generate no-more-business-as-usual.

The second priority of the no-more-business-as-usual paradigm is to lead your business with strategic awareness and prosperity consciousness, recognizing and benefiting from the connectedness and interdependence of all stakeholders. With strategic awareness you and your team will be able to know: "What are the biggest issues our organization needs to start addressing right now and what are the opportunities? What will change, and what will this mean for our business? What do we need to do about it and what actions do we need to be taking right now?" With this second priority you and your organization can become a catalyst to generate a prosperous world, one that can regenerate and rejuvenate itself, that nurtures generative societies and unified communities.

The third priority of the no-more-business-as-usual paradigm is you need to remove the ambiguity from your vision of change. You must have a clear vision of what would you really like to create and generate and what exactly you want to get out of this. You have to translate aspiration into new possibility by setting clear priorities for your business. You can accomplish this by utilizing creative business strategies that are both transformational and inspirational, ones that can help solve the world's many social and environmental problems, and create wealth for you. What is essential, though, is to marry your vision with your short-term critical action. You don't need to have a very specific action plan for each step on the journey between the current situation and your ultimate vision for your business to become a benevolent capitalist and to operate based on no-the-more-business-as-usual paradigm.

A New Way of Being

Throughout this book, we have shared our experience of what it takes for organizations to operate based on the no-more-business-as-usual paradigm. We have provided tools, inspiration, and transformational processes to help you to create the benevolent capitalism way of being for your business. We invite you to try these tools for yourself. The ideas we present may sound weird, wacky, or bizarre, but we have discovered for ourselves that they work. By making a deliberate choice to become a benevolent capitalist, you will set in motion the creation of your own reality and turn your business around.

We encourage you to take the ideas provided in this book and activate your awareness to perceive the possibilities that exist for all current businesses to relinquish outdated thinking and action. Our wish is that you will build upon the inspiration from this book for any future businesses or organizations you create as part of a new paradigm.

When the benevolent capitalism way of being is the primary state of your "beingness", you will be able to tap into deeper sources of possibility and create greater value for all stakeholders and the world. You will experience a knowing, confidence, gratitude, and certitude that all of your aspirations will be met—and this allows you to act more freely. When conscious leadership and the benevolent capitalism way of being is the primary state of your "beingness", you know everything is possible.

A major detriment to many people's health,
wealth, well-being and success is their fixed and
limited points of view of this finite reality.

Exciting Possibilities Are Underway

Recognizing a different possibility requires a different mindset and almost always demands a kind of awareness that is not part of prior experience. It takes an expanded zone of awareness to process complexity and deal with the ambiguity and abruptness of change.

Would you be willing to recognize that there is a vast realm of infinite intelligence beyond the mind and beyond thought? Are you willing to become aware of opportunity-maximizing and risk-minimizing strategies?

WHAT ELSE IS POSSIBLE?

If you've read *No More Business As Usual* and are choosing to have more, check out the resources we've created. All of these are free when you sign up for our mailing list. http://www.nomoreasusual.com/

On the site, you will be able to access more resources like:

- No More Business As Usual – for Personal Change

- No More Business As Usual – for the Social Sector

- No More Business As Usual – for Entrepreneurs

- Strategic Awareness: The Key to Personal Power

Please Join us on Facebook

http://www.facebook.com/NoMoreBusinessAsUsual

SPEAKING ENGAGEMENTS

Steven Bowman has given speeches to lots of different audiences—associations, businesses, and nonprofits. If you're interested in having Steve speak to your group, just send us a note about the event (date, location, audience, etc.):

steven@conscious-governance.com

WORKSHOPS & TRAINING

If you liked *No More Business As Usual* and would like more practice applying its concepts, we can work with you to design a workshop and training program for your organization, your leadership team, and your board. We can work with your team no matter where you are in the world.

If you want us to lead a workshop personally for your team, or to design a course for your organization, then send us a note:

steven@conscious-governance.com

REFERENCES AND FURTHER RESOURCES

Chapter 1

Gary Douglas, "Access Consciousness: The Ultimate Source for Change",
http://www.accessconsciousness.com/gary-douglas-story.asp

Peter Sheahan (2007). *Flip: How counter intuitive thinking is changing everything from branding and strategy to technology and talent*, Random House Australia

"Lou Gerstner's Turnaround Tales at IBM", Published: December 18, 2002 in Knowledge@Wharton,
http://knowledge.wharton.upenn.edu/article.cfm?articleid=695

Lisa DiCarlo, "How Lou Gerstner Got IBM To Dance",
http://www.forbes.com/2002/11/11/cx_ld_1112gerstner.html

Amy Harmon, "Powerful Music Software Has Industry Worried",
http://www.nytimes.com/library/tech/00/03/biztech/articles/07net.html

BBC News (2009). "Music industry 'missed' Napster",
http://news.bbc.co.uk/2/hi/technology/8120552.stm

Courtney Macavinta, Staff Writer, CNET (1999). "News Recording industry sues music start-up, cites black market",
http://news.cnet.com/Recording-industry-sues-music-start-up,-cites-black-market/2100-1023_3-234092.html

Paul Zane Pilzer (1991). *Unlimited Wealth: The Theory and Practice of Economic Alchemy*, Crown Publishing

Chapter 2

Gary Douglas, "Access Consciousness: The Ultimate Source for Change"
http://www.accessconsciousness.com/gary-douglas-story.asp

Paul B. Carroll, Chunka Mui (2008). *Billion Dollar Lessons*, Penguin Group

Chevron energy, Delivering Clean Energy,
http://www.chevron.com/globalissues/emergingenergy/

Alternative Energy (2007). "Oil companies Promote Alternative Energy",
http://www.alternative-energy-news.info/oil-companies-promote-alternative-energy/

Experiment Resource.com, "The Arch Experiment, A series of studies conducted by Solomon Asch",
http://www.experiment-resources.com/asch-experiment.html

Scientific America (1955). "Opinion and Social Pressure by Solomon E. Arch",
http://www.columbia.edu/cu/psychology/terrace/w1001/readings/asch.pdf

Geoffrey Smith, "Can George fisher fix Kodak?" Business Week, October 20, 1997, http://www.businessweek.com/1997/42/b3549001.htm

Bruce Upbin, "Kodak's Digital Moment", Forbes, August 21, 2000, http://www.forbes.com/forbes/2000/0821/6605106a.html

Michael Porter, *On competition.* (Boston: Harvard Business School Press, 1998)

Chapter 3

Chutisa Bowman, Steven Bowman, (2005). *Conscious Leadership,* LifeMastery Australia Pty. Ltd.
http://www.conscious-governance.com

Mahatma Gandhi Online, Mahatma Gandhi Biography, http://www.mahatmagandhionline.com/

Chapter 4

Chutisa Bowman, Steven Bowman, (2005). *Conscious Leadership,* LifeMastery Australia Pty. Ltd.,
http://www.conscious-governance.com

Frederic P. Miller (Editor), Agnes F. Vandome (Editor), John McBrewster (Editor) (2010). *Entrainment (Physics): Oscillation, Synchronous, Christian Huygens, Physicist, Pendulum clock, Negative feedback,* Resonance, Alphascript Publishing

Andrew Pavelski (2011). "Brainwave Entrainment History: The Evolution Of Brain Waves",
http://andrewpavelski.com/2011/08/24/brainwave-entrainment-history-the-evolution-of-brain-waves/

P. S. Spoor and G. W. Swift, (2000). "The Huygens entrainment phenomenon and thermoacoustic engines", http://www.lanl.gov/thermoacoustics/Pubs/JASA00Huygens.pdf

Chapter 5

Bill Strickland (2007). *Make the Impossible Possible. One Man's Crusade to Inspire Others to Dream Bigger and Achieve the Extraordinary.* Crown Business

Chapter 6

Warren Bennis (1994). *On Becoming A Leader.* Perseus Books; Rev/2nd edition

Jonas Salk. (n.d.). BrainyQuote.com. Retrieved November 26, 2011, from BrainyQuote.com Web site: http://www.brainyquote.com/quotes/authors/j/jonas_salk.html

Lynn B. Robinson (1994). *Coming Out of Your Psychic Closet: How to Unlock Your Naturally Intuitive Self.* Factor Pr Lynn B. Robinson, "Intuition in Business", http://www.theharbinger.org/xvii/981117/robinson.html

Debra Davenport, "Intuition often is your best weapon in business", http://davenportinstitute.com/component/content/article/25-library/113-intuition-your-best-weapon-in-business

LeDoux, J.E. (1996). *The Emotional Brain.* New York, Simon and Schuster.

LeDoux J.E. (2002). *Synaptic Self: How Our Brains Become Who We Are.* New York, Viking.

Berners-Lee, Tim; Mark Fischetti (1999). *Weaving the Web: The Original Design and Ultimate Destiny of the World Wide Web by its inventor.* Britain: Orion Business.

Tim Berners-Lee—Time 100 People of the Century. *Time Magazine.* "He wove the World Wide Web and created a mass medium for the 21st century. The World Wide Web is Berners-Lee's alone. He designed it. He loosed it on the world. And he more than anyone else has fought to keep it open, nonproprietary and free."

Berners Lee Long Biography World Wide Web Consortium. Retrieved 18 January 2011.

Bruce Upbin, "Kodak's Digital Moment", *Forbes*, August 21, 2000, http://www.forbes.com/forbes/2000/0821/6605106a.html

Chapter 7

Gary Douglas, "Access Consciousness: The Ultimate Source for Change", http://www.accessconsciousness.com/gary-douglas-story.asp

George Beahm (editor 2011). *iSteve. Steve Jobs in his own words.* Hardie Grant books

Academy of achievement, Sir Roger Bannister Biography, Track and Field Legend, Breaking the four minute mile, http://www.achievement.org/autodoc/page/ban0bio-1

History.com, Roger Bannister breaks four minutes mile, http://www.history.com/this-day-in-history/roger-bannister-breaks-four-minutes-mile

Chapter 8

Albert Einstein. BrainyQuote.com. Xplore Inc, 2011. 27 November. 2011.
http://www.brainyquote.com/quotes/authors/a/albert_einstein_2.html

The Matrix, a 1999 science fiction-action film written and directed by Larry and Andy Wachowski, starring Keanu Reeves, Laurence Fishburne, Carrie-Anne Moss, Joe Pantoliano, and Hugo Weaving. http://en.wikipedia.org/wiki/The_Matrix

Chutisa Bowman, Steven Bowman, (2005). *Conscious Leadership*. LifeMastery Australia Pty. Ltd. http://www.conscious-governance. com

Chapter 9

George Beahm (editor 2011). *iSteve. Steve Jobs in his own words.* Hardie Grant books

Ecomagination, The new ecomagination.com is a forum for fresh thinking and conversation about clean technology and sustainable infrastructure. http://www.ecomagination.com/about 2008 ecomagination Annual Report, Ecomagination is GE, http:// ge.ecomagination.com/_files/downloads/reports/ge_2008_ ecomagination_report.pdf

FedEx History in APAC, http://www.fedex.com/as/about/history.html

Academy of achievement, Father of the overnight delivery business, Frederick W Smith, http://www.achievement.org/autodoc/page/smi0int-1

Enron Federal Credit Union History, https://www.startrustfcu.com/about/history/

The Music industry for you, Struggle to maintain-status-quo, A case study of the music industry http://themusicindustry4you.blogspot.com/2011/09/struggle-to- maintain-status-quo-case.html

Devin Leonard (2003). "Songs In The Key Of Steve Steve Jobs may have just created the first great legal online music service. That's got the record biz singing his praises".
http://money.cnn.com/magazines/fortune/fortune_archive/2003/05/12/342289/index.htm

"CNN talks to Steve Jobs about iTunes", November 27, 2003,
http://articles.cnn.com/2003-04-29/tech/jobs.interview_1_music-service-music-store-song-swapping-services?_s=PM:TECH

The Economic Times, With iTunes Steve Jobs tuned music to consumer taste and helped control piracy,
http://economictimes.indiatimes.com/news/international-business/with-itunes-steve-jobs-tuned-music-to-consumer-taste-and-helped-control-piracy/articleshow/10294354.cms

Chapter 10

Jennifer Reingold (2005). "What P&G Knows About the Power of Design", Fast Company,
http://www.fastcompany.com/magazine/95/design-qa.html

A. G. Lafley, Ram Charan (2008). *The Game-Changer: How You Can Drive Revenue and Profit Growth with Innovation.* Crown Business

McKinsey Quarterly James Manyika (2008). "Google's view on the future of business: An interview with CEO Eric Schmidt, How the Internet will change the nature of competition, innovation, and company operations".
http://www.mckinseyquarterly.com/Googles_view_on_the_future_of_business_An_interview_with_CEO_Eric_Schmidt_2229

Mary Buffett, David Clark, (2006). "The Tao of Warren Buffett. Warren Buffett's Words of Wisdom: Quotations and Interpretations to Help Guide You to Billionaire Wealth and Enlightened Business Management". Scribner Publishing

Mary Buffett, David Clark, (2006). *Warren Buffett's Management Secrets: Proven Tools for Personal and Business Success.* Scribner Publishing

Research conducted by The Carnegie Institute of Technology, Carnegie Mellon University, 5000 Forbes Avenue, Pittsburgh, PA 15213 http://www.cit.cmu.edu/research/index.html

Branson, Richard (1999). Losing My Virginity: How I've Survived, Had Fun, And Made a Fortune Doing Business My Way. Three Rivers Press.

Branson, Richard (2007). *Screw It, Let's Do It Expanded: Lessons in Life and Business.* Virgin

Jennifer Reingols (2004). "Ram Charan - Man of Mystery", Fast Company, http://www.fastcompany.com/magazine/79/ram.html

David Whitford (2007). "The strange existence of Ram Charan", http://money.cnn.com/magazines/fortune/fortune_archive/2007/04/30/8405482/index.htm

Chas Newkey-Burden (2009). "Heston Blumenthal: The Biography of the World's Most Brilliant Master Chef". John Blake Publishing Ltd

Heston Blumenthal (2009). *Total Perfection: In Search of Total Perfection.* Bloomsbury Publishing PLC

Chapter 11

Paul B. Carroll, Chunka Mui (2008). *Billion Dollar Lessons.* Penguin Group

Steve Jobs: Stanford commencement address, June 2005, http://www.ted.com/talks/steve_jobs_how_to_live_before_you_die.html

Jeffrey H. Dyer, Hal B. Gregersen, and Clayton M. Christensen

(2009). "Spotlight on Innovation: The Innovator's DNA". Harvard Business Reviews, http://www.epicentret.dk/hbr.pdf

Peter Drucker (2006). *The Effective Executive: The Definitive Guide to Getting the Right Things Done.* Harper Paperbacks

Peter Drucker (2008). *The Five Most Important Questions You Will Ever Ask About Your Organization.* Jossey-Bass Publishing

Chapter 12

Charles Dickens (1986). *A Christmas Carol.* Bantam Classic

Josep Michelli (2006). *The Starbucks Experience: 5 Principles for Turning Ordinary Into Extraordinary.* McGraw-Hill

Howard Behar (2009), It's Not About the Coffee: Lessons on Putting People First from a Life at Starbucks, Portfolio Trade

Gary Hamel, Bill Breen (2009). *Creating a Community of Purpose: Whole Foods Market: Management Innovation in Action.* Harvard Business Press

Gary Hamel (2007). *The Future of Management.* Harvard Business School Publishing.

Citizens Engage - Edelman goodpurpose® Study2010, fourth annual global consumer survey, http://www.edelman.com/insights/special/GoodPurpose2010globalPPT_WEBversion.pdf

Hilborn, Robert C. (2004). "Sea gulls, butterflies, and grasshoppers: A brief history of the butterfly effect in nonlinear dynamics". American Journal of Physics 72 (4): 425–427. Bibcode 2004AmJPh..72..425H. doi:10.1119/1.1636492.

Butterfly effect, From Wikipedia, the free encyclopedia, http://en.wikipedia.org/wiki/Butterfly_effect

Robert Spector (1996). *The Nordstrom Way: The Inside Story of America's #1 Customer Service Company.* Wiley

Southern California Edison, "Energy Management Success Story: Nordstrom", http://asset.sce.com/Documents/Case%20Studies/NordstromCaseStudy.pdf

Leslie Guevarra (2010), "Nordstrom Opens New Chapter in Its Sustainability Story", Green Biz, http://www.greenbiz.com/blog/2010/12/23/nordstrom-opens-new-chapter-its-sustainability-story-0

Chutisa Bowman and Steven Bowman (2007). Prosperity Consciousness: *Leading yourself to money with conscious awareness.* iUniverse

Chapter 13

Rajendra S. Sisodia, David B. Wolfe and Jagdish N. Sheth (2007). *Firms of Endearment: How World Class Companies Profit from Passion and Purpose.* Wharton School Publishing.

ABOUT THE AUTHORS

About Chutisa and Steven Bowman

Chutisa and Steven Bowman are highly sought after advisors, facilitators, and speakers, well-known among CEOs, senior executives, and boards around the world for their uncanny ability for bringing the most complex problems down to the fundamentals from a very different point of view.

They are the new breed of business partners of the 21st century. In early 2000, both Chutisa and Steven quit their full-time senior executive positions to set up business advising and consulting to society-changing organizations. They chose to be together 24/7 and go everywhere and anywhere around the world in their quest to facilitate business leaders to lead with Strategic Awareness. They do this in a unique style that is exemplified by some interesting and unusual facts. They met as childhood sweethearts, have been married for 32 years, and have one daughter. They travel the world working together as an incredibly dynamic advisory team. Based in Australia, they spend up to 6 months of each year in different countries, working with leaders and boards of society-changing organizations.

Chutisa and Steven have a rare perspective on global leadership trends, having worked with clients in Australia, Asia, Europe, and North America. Their unique blend of gender and cross-cultural experiences has resulted in products and programs that facilitate leaders to lead with Strategic Awareness. They provide blended learning products, toolkits, workshops, and articles that have positioned them as thought leaders in these areas. They have currently exported information and blended learning products and services for society-changing CEOs and boards to the USA, Korea, Thailand, Singapore, Italy, Sweden, and the UK.

They have consulted to a wide range of commercial, professional, trade, welfare, philanthropic, and charitable organizations, and have authored or co-authored more than 14 books on governance and executive leadership. They currently work with more than 1,000 nonprofit and corporate organizations each year in Australia, New Zealand, USA, and Asia in governance, executive leadership, innovation, risk and generative edge strategic planning. They have also been invited to present at numerous international conferences. They have also been invited by the Australian Federal Government to participate in the Federal Austrade/TradeStart program to export their products and services worldwide.

What makes Chutisa and Steven so different and so highly sought after is their intensity of awareness and their combined amazing depth and breadth of experience, along with an innate ability to read the forces that shape the times in which we live and to seize on the resulting opportunities. They are widely regarded as the world's foremost authority on conscious governance and generative edge strategic planning. Many people have come to know them through in-house executive education programs. They bring a unique perspective to their work that merges personal awareness with executive level corporate skills. Their experience and career are vast and atypical.

Steve has held CEO positions with major organizations such as the Australasian Institute of Banking and Finance, the Finance and Treasury Association, CPA Australia, and has been a Director of the American College of Health Care Administrators. He has an extensive background in the nonprofit and society-changing arena. He is a past President of the Australian Society of Association Executives, and has held numerous other Board positions internationally. He pioneered the teaching of nonprofit management in Australia at the Monash/Mt Eliza Business School, one of the most prestigious business and MBA schools in the Southern Hemisphere, and taught there for 11 years. He has also lectured at Monash University, Melbourne University and has written a number of articles published by these institutions on the subject of strategy. Steve has been awarded the honor of Fellow of the Australian Institute of Company Directors and Fellow of the Corporate Law and Accountability Research Group at Monash University.

Chutisa has had an extraordinarily diverse life, from her beginnings in a traditional aristocratic family in Thailand to her remarkable rise through the executive ranks of the international business world to become a well-respected corporate leader, speaker, business consultant, workshop facilitator, and author. Her long, distinguished background includes prominent executive roles at numerous world-class companies, including senior executive for the Coles-Myer Corporation, Senior Buyer for K-Mart and the Target Retail Group, and Director of Buying for David Jones Department Store. Her leadership as a senior executive for the Coles-Myer Corporation, Australia's largest publicly listed corporation, was also exemplified by remarkable achievements in strategic retail developments and product ranges. She was responsible for successfully managing a $25 million budget annually. At each step of the way, she has developed her status as an accomplished strategist and effective leader.

Their target is to facilitate expansion of strategic awareness in the workplace and business arena, so that conscious awareness can spread throughout society and transform the world. They have focused on developing processes to help organizations build a culture of generative edge and strategically aware leadership teams. They use their own experience and many years of research to help CEOs, boards, and leadership teams expand their strategic awareness and change the culture of their workplace. Steve is trained in both organizational management and as a behavioral scientist. He received his undergraduate degree in applied science, speech pathology, from La Trobe University, where he also completed a post-graduate degree in communication disorders. He completed his master's degree from George Washington University, Washington DC, in speech pathology, where he also completed a master's degree in association management. He also earned a certificate in association management and an advanced certificate in association management at the Monash-Mt. Eliza Business School.

Chutisa is trained as both a transpersonal psychotherapist and conventional behavioral scientist and ergonomics. Chutisa received her undergraduate qualification from the IKON Institute in transpersonal counseling, her post-graduate degree from La Trobe University, Melbourne, Australia, in ergonomics/human factors, and a master's degree in counseling from Monash University, Melbourne, Australia. She has gone beyond her academic training, however, by acquiring a depth and breadth of knowledge in a number of fields, including ACCESS Energy for Transformation, behavioral medicine, stress and well-being, HeartMath processes, and meditation. She has also extensively studied consciousness, creativity, and the great spiritual traditions of the world.

Through working with top business leaders around the world for more than two decades, they have developed an expansive view of the global business landscape coupled with their own finely tuned business acumen. Steve has personally worked with some of the most respected executive leaders globally, including Robert Joss, now Dean of Stanford Business School, the CEOs of major international banks such as Wells Fargo Bank, the Commonwealth Bank of Australia, Westpac, National Bank of Australia, and ANZ Bank. Chutisa has worked as a senior consultant with one of Australia's most prominent usability and human factors specialist consulting firms. This gave her an opportunity to work extensively with organizations such as Telstra, Australia Post, ANZ Bank, CSIRO, Authentic8, Mercantile Mutual, and the Department of Education, Employment and Training-State of Victoria.

They have developed ConsciousGovernance.com (www.conscious-governance.com), an online resource for nonprofit boards and executive leadership teams, strategic awareness online blending learning programs. They provide useful tools and practical techniques to assist boards and their organizations to advance their governance practices from compliance to generative edge and innovative advantage. They help CEOs and boards:

Increase awareness to perceive and know future potential, the big picture and global trends

Discover hidden opportunities and generate increased revenue

Perceive risk as strategic advantage

Leverage unique capabilities that are responsive to rapidly changing environments

Enhance organizational culture and climate - Create a self sustaining culture of conscious strategic awareness.

Improve ability to communicate and relate with strategic awareness and enhance the organization's standing in the community

Build new levels of board and stakeholder engagement

Lead from the generative edge with awareness of future potential coupled with operational efficiency and effectiveness.

To find out more, please visit: www.conscious-governance.com

Lightning Source UK Ltd.
Milton Keynes UK
UKOW04f1437240914

239098UK00013B/399/P